Graham Greene
and Cinema

Graham Greene in Lecture at the National Film Theatre, London, 1970. Courtesy of The National Film Archive, Stills Department, England.

Graham Greene and Cinema

Judith Adamson

Pilgrim Books, Inc.
Norman, Oklahoma

Published by Pilgrim Books
P.O. Box 2399, Norman, Oklahoma 73070
Copyright © 1984 by Pilgrim Books, Inc.
All rights reserved
ISBN 0–937664–00–0

Printed and Bound in the United States of America
First Edition

Library of Congress Cataloging in Publication Data

Adamson, Judith.
    Graham Greene and cinema.

    Filmography
    Bibliography
    Includes index.
        1. Greene, Graham, 1904–   —Moving-picture plays.
2. Greene, Graham, 1904–   —Criticism and interpretation.
3. Moving-pictures and literature.   I. Title.
PR6013.R44Z59   1984   822'.912   [B]   84-12113
ISBN 0–937664–65–0

For Alan and Nicholas

Contents

Illustrations

Preface

This is a book about words and images, about Graham Greene's words and the visual images he and film makers have made from them. It is about the literary ideas he brought to his film work and the cinematic techniques he took from it to his fiction.

In acknowledging their debt to literary sources, both David Wark Griffith and Sergei Eisenstein discussed the bearing of literature on film, but critics have only recently begun to study the relationship with any intensity. Of the books written about the problem of changing fiction into film, George Bluestone's *Novels into Film* (1968), Claude-Edmonde Magny's *The Age of the American Novel* (1972), Edward Murray's *The Cinematic Imagination* (1972), Robert Richardson's *Literature and Film* (1969), and Geoffrey Wagner's *The Novel and the Cinema* (1975) remain among the best. Unfortunately, many others do little more than outline filmed stories and mention the novelists and playwrights who have, at one time or another, written for the cinema. This list is by now well known; it includes James Agee, William Faulkner, F. Scott Fitzgerald, Ernest Hemingway, Christopher Isherwood, John Osborne, Alain Robbe-Grillet, Jean-Paul Sartre, John Steinbeck, and Nathanael West.

Graham Greene was usually excluded from the discussion until 1972, when John Russell Taylor published a selection of his film criticism. The book added an important dimension to Greene's work, especially for those who were unfamiliar with his long-standing interest in film. Two years later Gene D. Phillips, S.J., wrote *Graham Greene: The Films of His Fiction* and edited an issue of *Literature/Film Quarterly* devoted to the subject. Phillips's book discussed the many plot differences between the novels and their film adaptations and gave us a chronology, if sometimes inaccurate, of Greene's long association with the film world. His book opened the way for other scholars, whose articles he subsequently collected.

It is difficult to understand why students of literature and film did not go on to consider this aspect of Greene's work with increasing seriousness, for he has been connected with more films than have most other major novelists, and his writing offers us an almost unparalleled opportunity to study what happens when the word is made flesh. Critics have referred to him as a cinematic writer, but few have tried to explain exactly what that means. Taylor has mentioned, as have many others, that Greene's novels have "close-ups" and "long-shots."[1] Phillips has said the stories are "crisply cut like cinema montage."[2] Yet these devices have been used by novelists for centuries and, as D. W. Griffith and Sergei Eisenstein both noted, are not cinematic techniques at all. They are literary ones that have found their way into filmic use.

On another tack, André Bazin has said readers can "visualize" Greene's stories.[3] Richard Hoggart pointed to the "visual quality of the scenes."[4] John Boulting wanted to film *Brighton Rock* because he could "see it."[5] Yet surely it is the purpose of novelist as well as cinematographer to "make the mind see."[6] That Greene's readers find his novels visual signifies their literary power, not necessarily their cinematic quality. Nevertheless, Greene's novels did change during the years he was a film critic (1935–40), and many of the writing techniques he adopted appear to have come from his exposure to film.

In his literary criticism of the 1930s he talked of his desire to "paint life as it is"[7] so that ordinary readers would recognize some common ground between themselves and what they read. He meant not that writers should emulate turn-of-the-century naturalism but that their art should reflect and analyze the world in which they lived. If an artist cut himself off from his audience, Greene thought, he lost the source of his inspiration and could not honestly consider "life as it is and life as it ought to be,"[8] that relationship between the objective outside world and the subjective individual world that is the subject of art.

As a young man Greene recognized the corruption of his society and knew the system had destroyed many of the values he held close. Yet as a writer he was not in a position to effect social change. He looked for another way he and other artists could touch the masses and found the cinema. Here, he felt, a writer could easily capture a large, undiscriminating public and present it with the truth.

His ideas about cinema were an extension of the novelist's commitment to popular art. He expounded them in his film criticism and went on to put them to the test in many movies. But, as John Grierson once said, "Great writers have had bad luck with the cinema,"[9] and Greene is no exception. Yet few have remained so continually occupied with film, and few have to their credit movies as undeniably excellent as *The Fallen Idol* and *The Third Man*.

Still it is difficult to measure Greene's place in cinema history, for although these two films are among the finest ever made in England, only one or two others of those with which he was associated approximate their excellence. It is equally troublesome to measure his proficiency as a film writer, for although the cinema has occupied a great deal of his time since 1932, it has never been his prime concern. It thus seems both unfair and fruitless to judge his work as one would that of a film maker.

If, however, we use his own critical criteria to examine his film work and consider the effect of that work on his novels, we see that his place in cinema history is not unimportant. That Greene has contributed to some successful films makes the study of his cinema work more interesting, but not necessarily more rewarding. What is important is not that his scripts have made great movies—good scripts have, after all, become bad movies, and bad scripts, good ones—but that he took the film seriously. Because of this his work offers an extraordinary opportunity: as one of the few major novelists to write for and about the cinema, his criticism and scripts facilitate the study of one of the major aesthetic problems of our century: the nature of and difference between the verbal and visual media.

Parts of chapters 1 and 3 of this book have been rewritten from "Graham Greene as Film Critic" and "Looking for the Third Man," which originally appeared in *Sight and Sound* (Spring, 1972) and *Encounter* (June, 1978), respectively. I thank the editors of those journals for permission to use this material.

I wish to thank the Canada Council for travel and research funds; the British Film Institute for procuring prints of Greene's films and arranging for me to view them; and the staffs of the British Film Institute Library, the British Library and its Newspaper Library at Colindale, the Humanities Research Center at the University of Texas, Austin, and Beryl Moser, at the Dawson College Library for their help.

I am indebted to Alan Adamson, Penelope Houston, Philip Stratford, and Joan Worley for their critical comments; to John Boulting and the late John Grierson for granting me interviews; and to Jay Allen, Neil Brennan, the late Alan Redway, and the late Paul Rotha for correspondence that provided me with essential information.

I am particularly grateful to Graham Greene for the two interviews I had with him, for his generous help in reading over the manuscript, and for his permission to quote liberally from his work.

Montreal   Judith Adamson

1

The
Critical
Years

In July, 1935, Graham Greene became cinema critic for the *Spectator*. Each day for the next four and a half years he opened "the envelopes, which contained the gilded cards of invitation for the morning Press performances . . . with a sense of curiosity and anticipation." As an undergraduate he had previously written a few articles on film for the *Oxford Outlook*. The idea of reviewing films professionally came to him "at a cocktail party after the dangerous third martini. . . . [He] was talking to Derek Verschoyle, the Literary Editor of the *Spectator*. The *Spectator* had hitherto neglected films" and Greene suggested he "should fill the gap." At the time he never imagined the job would remain fun for long. But it did, and ended only when he had seen more than four hundred films, in March, 1940, in "a different world, a world at war."[1]

During his tenure as reviewer Greene wrote four novels and a travel

1

book. The films, he says, "were an escape—escape from that hellish problem of construction in Chapter Six, from the secondary character who obstinately refused to come alive, escape for an hour and a half from the melancholy which falls inexorably round the novelist when he has lived for too many months on end in his private world."[2] Yet he took the cinema seriously enough to write pieces on it for *Fortnightly Review*, the *Times* (London), *World Film News*, and *Sight and Sound*, as well as his regular *Spectator* column, and to assume the additional role of film critic (he was also coeditor) for the weekly *Night and Day* from July to December, 1937.

What distinguished his criticism was its bite and wit. He wrote, when reviewing *A Midsummer Night's Dream*:

> I sometimes wonder whether film reviewers are taken quite seriously enough. Criticism, of course, may not be quite in our line, but the production of *A Midsummer Night's Dream* has demonstrated beyond doubt that no one can shake a better tambourine or turn a better table. We are superb mediums, or is it an intuitive sympathy with the poet which enables Mr. Luscombe Whyte . . . to tell us that Shakespeare "had he lived now" would have approved of Herr Reinhardt's film version of his play? . . . Alas! I failed to get in touch with Shakespeare . . . but I feel quite sure that Anne Hathaway, "had she lived now," would have thought this a very nice film (I am uncertain of the Dark Lady of the Sonnets).[3]

Clearly Greene had no sympathy for his colleagues who wrote for the middle class. Nor had he any for the escapist film that catered to its tastes: "Millions go to the cinema, but do they really get what *they* want or do they get what the middle class public wants?—the cinema of escape. The thousands who come down to Wembley . . . don't want to escape. They want something as simple and exciting as a cup-tie, just as the Elizabethan public wanted something as brutal and exciting as what went on in the bear-pit."[4] The cinema should belong to them, and "any artist who rejects the ivory tower, who wants his art to be part of the vulgar natural life"[5] should welcome the chance to work for it.

Greene's interest in creating a really popular art did not begin with his work as a cinema critic, nor was it unique to himself. He belonged to that generation of modern British writers who found themselves as young men caught between the moral vacuity of a decaying liberal world and the threat of totalitarianism. In his earliest rememberings we find him nostalgic for the relative peace and security of the middle class Edwardian world of his childhood. But even in that childhood a note of uneasiness is heard. Even then Greene had experienced that perplexity of border crossings which he would later employ in his fiction with such metaphoric power. "If," he said, remembering himself as the son of the headmaster at Berkhamsted School, "you pushed open a green baize door in a passage by my father's study, you entered another passage deceptively similar, but none-the-less you were on alien ground."[6] This in 1939. Thirty-two years later, recalling the same experience, he continued, "I had left civilization behind and entered a savage country of strange customs and inexplicable cruelties."[7] This sense of sudden transition extended to early childhood forays into Berkhamsted, where he was away from his mother, who "seemed to eliminate all confusion, to recognize the good from the bad and choose the good."[8] Alone, he discovered that "appalling cruelties could be practised. . . . no one really was responsible for anyone else."[9]

Even at Christmas the young Greene entered a "region of extremes"[10] when his branch of the family, the "intellectual Greenes," visited the "rich Greenes" living in "the Hall, the great house of the town."[11] The subtle difference in circumstance of the two families indicates an early understanding of the "intellectual Greenes' " position at the lower edge of the ruling class. Greene stood to inherit no substantial property. He would rely on a profession for his living and be dependent on the system that, even as a boy, he had come to suspect. On his solitary childhood walks and within his father's schoolhouse the young Greene saw things that contradicted what his liberal Edwardian upbringing had led him to expect. And so the loss of childhood brought with it a sharp intimation of cruelty and latent social disorder existing beyond the secure borders of family life.

The young writer's uneasiness at crossing these early frontiers developed into an overriding preoccupation with the discrepancy between the old liberal myths that had ruled the world of his childhood and what his keen eye showed him they had wrought. How often he has paraphrased Chekhov: "I find myself always torn between two beliefs: the belief that life should be better than it is and the belief that when it appears better it is really worse."[12]

When faced with what Christopher Isherwood called "the fantastic realities"[13] of the 1930s—the confusion of values, the rise of fascism, the fear of a coming war, the Depression, the pervading sense of losing control to a rapacious capitalism—Greene felt at the end of an age. "Centuries of cerebration" he believed, had brought man only to "unhappiness" and the "peril of extinction."[14]

Yet whereas Christopher Isherwood, Stephen Spender, Edward Upward, C. Day Lewis, John Cornford, and many other young writers sought a new direction in socialism, Greene submerged himself in "the seediness of civilisation" and the "darkness" of Africa and Mexico in search of another bearing. The topography of his novels during the thirties reflects his desire to withdraw from his own intellectual and bourgeois background and to examine man "nearer the beginning."[15] *Journey Without Maps* is, as Samuel Hynes noted in *The Auden Generation*, a kind of Jungian voyage into the self and the racial memory. *A Gun for Sale* and *Brighton Rock* were presented as "Entertainments" set in seedy contemporary England, but are in fact symbolic moral novels that penetrate the heart of a society on the verge of war.

Greene wanted to explore "one's place in time, based on a knowledge not only of one's present but of the past from which one has emerged." This did not mean based on a knowledge of conventional history. In *Journey Without Maps* he explained that as psychoanalysis brings the patient back to the idea which he is repressing, one might find "one's place in time" by moving backward through the three levels of human development: the civilized, the seedy or semicivilized, and the primitive. If one explored the collective unconscious in this way, discovering "from what we have come," one might discover "at which point we went astray."[16]

Greene's early interest in melodrama and his initial excitement about film as a popular art must be seen in the light of this overriding concern that a direction for the future be found elsewhere than in his own decaying bourgeois culture. His attention to detail in the seedy marginal world of his early novels and his relentless pursuit of the correlation between sociological and psychological phenomena cannot be separated from his desire to examine the minutiae of the places in which he sought an answer to civilization's problems.

In the cinema of the thirties Greene confronted Britain's populace, the mass who came to be excited and entertained. In a sense the cinema allowed him to do what George Orwell and other writers of their generation attempted: to cross the border of his own social position and reach those whose lives his class controlled. W. H. Auden talked of writing "the thoughts of a wise man in the speech of the common people",[17] Greene, of creating "a new kind of art"[18] in the cinema that would begin at "the level of *The Spanish Tragedy*" and move "towards a subtler, more thoughtful level"[19] where human values could be suggested.

He had always believed the best English drama to be rooted in common experience. "Shakespeare had belonged to the people, catching for the first time in verse the accent of common speech, giving them the violent, universal tragedies they understood." He and Ben Jonson had "served the people and the people had moulded them."[20] Even in his early literary essays Greene had given critical attention to many popular writers—Marjorie Bowen, A. J. Cronin, Arthur Conan Doyle, W. Somerset Maugham, Edgar Wallace—and had called for young authors to follow their direction. He himself had pursued a form of popular melodrama from his first stories, published in the *Berkhamstedian*, the *Weekly Westminster Gazette*, and the *Graphic* between 1920 and 1929, through the six novels that appeared before 1935. In these he had attempted to touch the average reader by giving him what *he* could recognize, as Shakespeare had the "men and women who watched from their windows the awful ritual of the scaffold" by responding with "the *exact* expression of a mental state: the *exact* description of a scene."[21]

The problem was that by 1935 Greene had learned that most popular writers could not match his own verbal accuracy. Indeed, he had "almost given up hope of hearing *words* with a vivid enough imagery to convey the climate of the drama."[22] He believed it easier to work in pictures than in words anyway, and so used his weekly film columns to encourage on screen the realism he rarely found in popular writing of the period.

First, he wrote, the film maker had to involve his audience in the popular drama. To do this, he advised film makers, they should consider the problem of providing the masses with what they wanted. The twentieth-century artist "will no longer be heartened by the direct applause, or criticised by the direct disapproval, of the common people. He will hear only the crackle of chocolate paper, the whispers of women with shopping baskets, the secret movements of courting couples."[23] The artist should take heed of these crackles and whispers and realize that they exist because he has not given his audience what it wanted. It does not "ask to be soothed: it asks to be excited," to be aroused like an Elizabethan audience, in communal response. This, he said, was "not the sum of private excitements, but mass feeling, mass excitement, the Wembley roar."[24]

Greene knew that the cinema, like the sports spectacle, is a physical medium. Film makes a direct impact on the audience. The response of an isolated reader or a theatergoer, separated from the actors by the footlights, is not the same as that of the film viewer. Hidden in a crowd, a film spectator watches from a darkened room. He identifies with what he sees, experiencing vicariously those emotions played out before him. If the film maker knew what he was about, Greene felt, he could use this intimacy to draw his audience into such mass excitement as that of Wembley or such mass feeling as that of the Elizabethan theater. Once he had done so, he could begin subtly to put over what he would "of horror, suffering, truth"[25] and allow his audience glimpses of the poetic that had been withheld from the common people since the Puritans closed the theaters.

Examples of films that aroused this kind of communal feeling were difficult to find. Greene cited "*Duck Soup*, the early Chaplins, a few 'shorts' by Laurel and Hardy, . . . perhaps *Fury, Le Million, Men and Jobs*. . . . These do convey the sense that the picture has been made by its spectators and not merely shown to them, that it has sprung, as much as their sports, from *their* level."[26]

It was toward the definition of this popular "poetic cinema"[27] that Greene devoted much of his time as film critic. Ford Madox Ford had divided fiction into novels and nuvvels (those stories he did not consider art). Greene followed suit, dividing films into cinema and movies. The latter represented the commercial escapist film. The former held greater possibilities, and it was here that he began his analysis of the poetic cinema. Like so many of his ideas about the novel, this consideration was influenced by Anton Chekhov, rooted as it was in the realization that the only subject matter for art was "life as it is: life as it ought to be." To be valid, art had to hold this antithesis. On film this meant that every poetic image should be "chosen for its contrasting value."[28]

Using *We from Kronstadt* as an example, he talked of "the gulls sweeping and coursing above the cliffs where the Red prisoners are lined up for their death by drowning, the camera moving from the heavy rocks around their necks to the movement of the light white wings."[29] Juxtaposing images of peace and freedom with those of war and death, and camera showed life as it ought to be—life as it was, gaining immense poetic power from the contrast.

Greene was defining something more aesthetic than cinematic here, for he was talking about a picture of reality as incomplete without its obverse—what ought to be. The Chekhov he paraphrased had its origin in chapter 25 of Aristotle's *Poetics*. "Since the poet," Aristotle wrote, ". . . is an imitator, he must always imitate some one of the three aspects of things: either as they were or are, or as men say they are and they seem to be, or as they ought to be."[30] Greene wanted to juxtapose Aristotle's "aspects of things" and form a philosophic montage between empirical reality and the artist's imagination, in filmic terms, between what was before the camera and what the artist felt were human possibilities.

Although he did not discuss the technical elements of these contrasting images, he made it quite clear that they were the combination of more than photography and cutting: "Photography by itself cannot make poetic cinema. . . . it can only make arty cinema. *Man of Aran* was a glaring example of this: how affected and wearisome were those figures against the skyline, how meaningless the magnificent photography of storm after storm."[31] Meaning came only with "the indications of life as it should be, the personal lyric utterance."[32]

Poetic cinema need not be complex. It could be "built up on a few simple ideas, as simple as the ideas behind the poetic fictions of Conrad: the love of peace, of country, a feeling for fidelity: it doesn't require a great mind to conceive them, but it does require an imaginative mind to feel them with sufficient passion. . . . Simple, sensuous and passionate, that definition would not serve the cinema badly."[33] Grigori Alexandrov's *Jazz Comedy* had this quality. Greene spoke of its "almost ecstatic happiness, . . . its sense of good living that owed nothing to champagne or women's clothes." He rejoiced in its "simple irrelevance, . . . its wildness, its grotesqueness.[34] Charlie Chaplin had 'a few simple ideas', . . . courage, loyalty, labour: against the . . . nihilistic background of purposeless suffering. . . . He doesn't try to explain, but presents with vivid fantasy what seems to him a crazy comic tragic world without a plan."[35]

Of the films Greene reviewed, few satisfied these rigorous criteria. Some, like *Dodsworth*, were partly successful. They had "the great

virtues of natural acting and natural speech," presenting life as it is,
in this case as it appears to an American millionaire. But they did not
show life as it ought to be. *Dodsworth*'s version of that was "a quaint
Italian villa on the bay of Naples and the company of a gentle, refined
and flower-like widow."[36] A little bourgeois for Greene's taste.

There were many other such examples. Cecil B. De Mille handled
an army of extras on the big sets as no other director did, creating a
sense of reality that was horrifyingly true to life. Yet in all but *The
Plainsman* these flashes of brilliant detail lasted only minutes in very
long films. Perry Mason, as played by Warren William, was Greene's
favored film detective because he was "cadaverous and not very well
dressed." Greene found him "real in his seedy straw hat with his
straggly moustache; . . . by no means irresistible to women; his
background . . . the hiss of soda rather than the clink of ice. . . . he
belongs to the same class as his criminals."[37] In *Poppy*, W. C. Fields's
complete dishonesty afforded a portrayal as vivid as that of any
Dickensian character. But all these films lacked that "critical purpose" that made the cinema poetic. The "sense of life as it should be"
was not there, and that sense, which "must always be a critical
one,"[38] was as important to the poetic cinema, and to all art, as the
sense of how life was. Perhaps it was even more important. It was
certainly more difficult to capture, for it meant that a director had to
analyze his material, making it transcend its actuality.

In his search for examples of poetic cinema Greene returned again
and again to Basil Wright's *Song of Ceylon*. "Faulty in continuity as it
was," it contained "criticism implicit in its images, life as it is
containing the indications of life as it should be."[39] Criticism implicit in the images—here was the essence of Greene's cinematic
canon. In *We from Kronstadt*, the scene he had described juxtaposed
two contrasting shots (one of life as it ought to be, the other of life as
it was), making one poetically whole image. The freedom of the birds
was as much a part of the execution sequence as were the stones
around the prisoners' necks. Without both, the sequence lost its
meaning, just as a linguistic trope does when one separates its parts.
The two shots are inextricably fused in the one image, producing a
complete vision of reality.

The reason Greene disliked *Man of Aran*, and most of Robert
Flaherty's other work, was that he did not find this kind of philosophical montage in its images, a montage that was above all dramatic. Flaherty tried to create such dramatic sequences artificially. In

this instance he had taught the young men of Aran to shark-hunt. To Greene's realist eye this was unnecessary, for the drama of poetic contrast was implicit in the lives of the people of Aran. Flaherty did not need to create it by manipulating their lives; he merely needed to capture it in the critical sense Greene had spoken of.

What Greene was asking of the camera was that it not lie. In *The Innocent Eye*, Arthur Calder-Marshall quotes Flaherty as saying that "sometimes you have to lie. . . . one often has to distort a thing to catch its true spirit."[40] Greene disagreed. Its true spirit was not in this kind of distortion but rather in the critical juxtaposition. This does not mean that he asked film to present a slice of life. He asked of it an honest but critical and poetic representation of reality. He did not believe the audience could be fooled by Flaherty's kind of distortion.

In contrast Greene offered Armand Denis's *Dark Rapture*, a film about Africa from which one carried away "a sense of innocence, of human dignity reduced to its essentials, . . . what Africa was before the white man came,"[41] and George Hoellering's *Hortobagy*, a film about the Hungarian plains acted by peasants and shepherds.

It was only when the audience recognized "the truth of a general scene" that it was "prepared to accept the truth of the individual drama,"[42] and as a novelist Greene knew very well that it was the individual drama that expanded the consciousness of the audience. "None of us believes very deeply in news, . . . the big events, the march of an army corps and the elimination of a people."[43] What makes us believe is a sense of involvement, which it was the camera's job to facilitate by noting with precision and vividness an atmosphere that would "give the story background and authenticity."[44]

He found Carol Reed particularly good at this: Reed's camera went "behind the dialogue, . . . [acting] with a kind of quick shrewd independence, . . . [presenting] its own equally dramatic commentary, so that the picture [here of suburbia in *Laburnum Grove*] seems to be drawn simultaneously from two angles." The detail picked up by Reed's camera, and the authenticity of the atmosphere it created, impressed Greene. Little did he know in 1936, when he concluded his review saying, "Mr. Reed, when he gets the script right, will prove far more than efficient"[45] that he himself would be providing the script, in fact two of them: *The Fallen Idol* (1948) and *The Third Man* (1949).

From these few examples one might suspect that Greene's sympathies lay with the documentary movement and that he most often found cinema to be poetic in the images created under its auspices. It is true that he repeatedly praised John Grierson and the General Post Office Unit, listing several of its films among his favorites; but they were not the majority on that list, which included, among others, Alberto Cavalcanti's *Rien Que Les Heures*, Arthur Robison's *Schatten*, Vsevolod Pudovkin's *Mother*, Charlie Chaplin's *The Gold Rush*, Erich von Stroheim's *Foolish Wives*, René Clair's *The Ghost Goes West*, Pierre Chenal's *Crime et Châtiment*, and Sergei Eisenstein's *October*. He realized the exclusiveness of documentary, that with "the subsidised film, we are getting far from the commercial picture." Unlike Grierson, he felt that such films would "always stand outside the ordinary cinema."[46] He did, however, continually use the documentary's simple honesty to emphasize by contrast the pretensions of the feature film.

Thus he attacked the star system, which stabilized the audience's attention on the star rather than on the film, allowing cheap, shoddy work to pass unnoticed. Similarly he spoke against the long film, which usually had to be padded to fill two hours. He complained about the gaudiness of color, asserting that it "would put film back technically twelve years."[47] But realizing that it had come to stay, he insisted that a way be found to use it "realistically, not only as a beautiful decoration." Stating that it must "be made to contribute to our sense of truth," he asked "can technicolour reproduce with the necessary accuracy the suit that has been worn too long, the oily hat?"[48]

Greene's choice of actors was also influenced by this concern for realism. Ingrid Bergman's first appearance in *Escape to Happiness* was one that "doesn't give the effect of acting at all, but of living." She was "natural as her name, . . . with a high-light gleaming on her nose-tip."[49] With Greta Garbo "you get an impression of immense force in reserve, an unexpressed passion of life. It is a quality of character rather than of acting. . . . Neither Garbo nor [Paul] Muni acts in this sense; they exist vividly and without apparent effort."[50]

It was this same criterion which led him to praise French films for using realism more imaginatively than did their British and American counterparts. So important was realism to him that he feared any attempt to use montage universally, even though it would instantly raise the standard of film production, because he felt that it would keep the mind "at too high a tension, . . . [not allowing] for the non-vital moments"[51] of life to be shown.

Such montage was unfaithful and contrary to Greene's artistic credo, which was to be "realistic and paint life as it is"[52]—to tell the truth. By truth he meant

> accuracy. . . . It is my duty to society not to write: "I stood above a bottomless gulf" or "going downstairs, I got into a taxi," because these statements are untrue. . . . we already see the effect of the popular novel on popular thought. Every time a phrase like one of these passes into the mind uncriticized, it muddies the stream of thought.[53]

Greene's pursuit of syntactical accuracy was central to his own and his generation's belief that the artist must address himself to what the audience could recognize. Stephen Spender discussed this relationship between the writer's and the audience's experience of reality more generally in *The New Realism* in 1939. He wrote:

> There is a tendency for artists today to turn outwards to reality, because the phase of experimenting in form has proved sterile. . . . the artist is simply in search of inspiration, having discovered that inspiration depends on there being some common ground of understanding between him and his audience about the nature of reality, and on a demand from that audience for what he creates.[54]

What the audience wanted was what it could understand, not what an artist who kept himself aloof from ordinary affairs produced, which was often "esoteric work, . . . frivolously decorative or elaborately erudite."[55]

Here we see an acute awareness of the reciprocal influence of the artist and the audience on each other. Isherwood believed that the artist might examine people at the movies "as though they were insects. . . .viewed from this standpoint, the stupidest film may be full of interesting revelations about the tempo and dynamics of everyday life: you see how actions look in relation to each other; how much space they occupy and how much time."[56] The artist may become the camera, he thought, "with its shutter open, quite passive, recording, not thinking."[57]

Greene too knew the value of watching his audience. Many years later, when receiving the Shakespeare Prize at the University of Hamburg, he said, ". . . the novelist's task is to draw his own likeness to any human being, . . . to roam through any human mind."[58] As a

young film critic of the 1930s he had put it more functionally. The
film maker's task was to observe his audience in order to catch its
likeness and use it to shake "the common people out of their indifference."[59] Even the film reviewer should "make a flank attack
upon the reader, to persuade him to laugh at personalities, stories,
ideas, methods, he has previously taken for granted."[60] If film
makers and critics took this responsibility seriously, then the cinema
would become a place of poetry with the power to suggest human
values, a place where ordinary people might roam with the artist
"through any human mind."

As critic Greene never veered from his original intentions for the
cinema. His lack of compromise was well known in the film world.
He belonged to no school and regarded nothing as sacred. With equal
acidity he attacked his fellow critics and Hollywood films. The
former were corrupt. The latter were "vulgar as only the great New
World can be vulgar, with the vulgarity of the completely un-
religious, of sentimental idealism, of pitchpine ethics, with the
hollow optimism about human nature of a salesman who has never
failed to sell his canned beans."[61] The Hollywood product emphasized "the eternal adolescence of the American mind, to which
literature means the poetry of Longfellow and morality means keeping Mother's Day and looking after the kid sister's purity."[62] "Occa-
sionally," he wrote, "a film of truth and tragic value gets somehow
out of Hollywood onto the screen. Nobody could explain it—perhaps
a stage needs using, all the big executives are in conference over the
latest Mamoulian 'masterpiece'—Jehovah was asleep, and when he
wakes he finds he's got a *Fury* on his hands, worse still *They Won't
Forget*."[63] "What's the use in pretending," Greene added, while
reviewing *The Road Back*, "that with these allies it was ever possible
to fight for civilisation? For Mother's Day, yes, for anti-vivisection
and humanitarianism, the pet dog and the home fire, for the co-ed
college and the campus. Civilisation would shock them: eyes on the
guide book for safety, they pass it quickly as if it were a nude in a
national collection."[64]

His bête noire in England was the Board of Film Censors, "which
allows a far greater latitude to the big American companies than to its
own less wealthy countrymen."[65] His last and perhaps most telling
attack against the board came in 1940, when it gave *The Wizard of Oz*
an A certificate, for "adults only." "Surely," he wrote, "it is time that

this absurd committee of elderly men and spinsters who feared, too, that *Snow-White* was unsuitable for those under sixteen, was laughed out of existence?"[66]

Only once were his remarks repressed and then on legal, not aesthetic, grounds. The incident arose over his October 28, 1937, review of the Shirley Temple film *Wee Willie Winkie*, which appeared in his regular column in *Night and Day*, a kind of Londoner's *New Yorker* designed to dislodge *Punch*. The weekly listed among its columnists, in addition to Graham Greene, Elizabeth Bowen, who reviewed plays, and Evelyn Waugh, who did books. Reviewing *Captain January* the previous year in the *Spectator*, Greene had written that Shirley Temple's popularity "seems to rest on a coquetry quite as mature as Miss[Claudette] Colbert's [in *Under Two Flags*] and on an oddly precocious body as voluptuous in grey flannel trousers as Miss [Marlene] Dietrich's."[67] This review seems to have caused no comment. The *Wee Willie Winkie* review was another matter. Shirley Temple (then aged eight) and 20th Century–Fox sued Greene; *Night and Day*; Hazell, Watson and Viney, Ltd. (the magazine's printer); and Chatto and Windus (its publisher) for libel, in a case that appeared before the King's Bench on March 22, 1938.

The review, which cannot be quoted here, was described by Sir Patrick Hastings, counsel for the plaintiffs, as "such a beastly libel to have written that if it had been a question of money it would have been difficult to say what would be an appropriate amount to arrive at."[68] Godfrey Winn, writing in the *Daily Mirror*, thought it "a queer review, because it was not a criticism of Shirley's clever acting at all, but one which introduced potential audience reactions— reactions which were entirely alien to Shirley's lovable and innocent humour."[69] *Night and Day* had in the meantime ceased publication, the issue in question having been withdrawn from the newsstands, and Greene had left for Mexico after being assured by his lawyer, Valentine Holmes, that his name would not come up at the hearing.[70]

However, it did. In a rather comic sequence the judge asked repeatedly where Greene was, and Holmes repeatedly answered that he had no information on the subject. Holmes apologized (in order that the record be withdrawn) to Shirley Temple "for the pain which would certainly have been caused to her by the article if she had read it" and to the two film companies (20th Century–Fox Film Corporation and 20th Century-Fox Film Company, Ltd.) "for the suggestion that they would produce and distribute a film of the character indicated in the article."[71] The *Wee Willie Winkie* libel case put the already financially ailing *Night and Day* out of business and reinforced the coffers of Shirley Temple, the film corporation and the film company to the tune of £2,000, £1,000, and £500, respectively.

The suit, however, had little effect on Greene's film criticism, whatever embarrassment and inconvenience it may have caused. His trip to Mexico, commissioned earlier by the publisher Longmans, Green, which wanted a report on religious persecution there, was unhampered. Later in 1938, when he returned to London, he began writing again for the *Spectator*, and although Basil Wright had taken over as film critic, Greene continued to review movies intermittently well into 1940, when he became their theater reviewer.

During the years he was cinema critic, the British film industry reached maturity. At the end of World War I it had fallen badly behind Hollywood. Its movies did not match the high technical standards of American films, and they were financially unsuccessful. Moreover, the practice of block booking, which was well established in England by the mid-1920s, made it difficult for British producers to exhibit their films at all. Indeed, by 1925 the situation was so bad that it was estimated that 95 percent of screen time in Britain was taken up by the American product.

To protect the British industry, the Cinematograph Films Act was passed in 1927. The act rigidly curtailed block booking and imposed a quota on the proportion of screen time to be given to English films (5 percent in 1928, rising annually to 20 percent in 1936). The effect was immediate. Although the advent of sound, which appeared just before the act came into effect, threw the entire industry into turmoil, the number of features made in England rose from 26 in 1926 to 128 in 1929. By 1934 it was up to 190 and in 1936 reached a pre–World War II peak at 212.

When Greene became film critic, the technical and aesthetic problems faced in the early years of sound had been overcome. Several first-rate British directors had emerged. In the early thirties Alfred Hitchcock and Anthony Asquith were the most respected entertainment film makers, but by the middle of the decade several new directors had become prominent. Michael Powell, Victor Saville and Carol Reed were among them. John Grierson's documentary movement had flourished under the auspices of the General Post Office. Alexander Korda's *The Private Life of Henry VIII* (1933) had broken into the lucrative American market. Thus despite the innumerable cheap films being made to satisfy the quota and allow English distributors to show profitable American movies, the British industry appeared to be on its feet.

Several kinds of entertainment films were being produced. In an attempt to duplicate *Henry VIII*'s triumph in America, millions of pounds were spent on lavish costume pieces. Paul Czinner made *Catherine the Great* (1934); Korda, *The Private Life of Don Juan* (1934) and *Rembrandt* (1936); and Victor Saville, *The Love Affair of the Dictator* (1935) and *The Iron Duke* (1935). Unfortunately, the success of these high-cost spectaculars depended on American distribution, which was not achieved despite the elaborate costumes and sets these movies sported. But film makers pressed on with more indigenously interesting films. Flaherty's *Man of Aran* appeared in 1934, Hitchcock's thrillers *The Man Who Knew Too Much* and *The Thirty-nine Steps* in 1935, and Reed's adaptation of J. B. Priestly's *Laburnum Grove* and Korda's of H. G. Wells's *Things to Come* in 1936.

In 1938 the Cinematograph Films Act was revised to stop production of what had come to be called "quota quickies." The revised act obliged producers to spend more on labor costs (£1 per foot, or at least £7,500 per film). Films costing between £22,555 and £37,500 in labor were granted two quota counts, and films over £37,500 were given three. With more money per reel to spend, film makers had time to perfect their pictures, and the quality of production rose. The revised act allowed short and feature films to be separately considered for quota status. This was important to the documentary movement, whose films had often been overlooked for commercial screening when they lacked quota qualification.

Although the industry was far from financially stable, in the last years of the decade it reached full height. Documentaries flourished, giving Britons films that informed and enlightened them. Their contribution to the cinema was well recognized, and the movement became so firmly a part of British film making that it spread from the G.P.O. group to form many independent documentary units. In its wake the best entertainment films looked increasingly at the British character and institutions. Reed's *Bank Holiday* (1938) studied the English working class on holiday. Saville's *South Riding* (1938) was an adaptation of Winifred Holtby's story of local English politics. Robert Stevenson's *Owd Bob* (1938) was a character study of an old Scottish shepherd.[72]

By the time Greene left his post as cinema critic, a genuine school of British film had emerged, with new directors, actors, and technicians who were skilled in their observations of English life. Reviewing Arthur Wood's *They Drive by Night* in 1939, Greene wrote: " . . . the resurrection of the English film continues. . . . the author . . . has taken characters in a simple melodramatic situation and given them a chance to show with some intensity their private battlefields."[73] In short, "English films . . . [were] becoming—English."[74]

As the industry changed and matured during the five years Greene was film critic, so his own novels underwent a metamorphosis. His first three books, and indeed the two he wrote and could not publish before them, were, like the mid-decade costume pieces of the film industry, historical romances. Perhaps, he speculates, he picked this genre because he "knew too little of the contemporary world to treat it. . . . the past was more accessible because it was contained in books."[75]

In his first unpublished novel, a black child born of white parents found "a kind of content by joining a ship at Cardiff as a Negro deckhand, so escaping from the middle class and his sense of being an outsider." In the second, a book that took off from John Carlyle's *Life of John Sterling*, "another young Englishman, anxious, like the black boy, to escape from his class, becomes involved in plots against the Spanish Government." His first published novel, *The Man Within* (1929), took "a small jump back in time from the days of the Carlist refugees to the days of smugglers in Sussex."[76] Although the second and third, *The Name of Action* (1930) and *Rumour At Nightfall* (1931), had political themes, both were fantasy. Even *Stamboul Train* (1932), for which Greene got the idea from the film *Grand Hotel*, had only a tenuous relation to historical reality.

It was not until 1934, in *It's a Battlefield*, that Greene began to write those intensely social novels for which he became famous during the first phase of his career. The novels of that early period, which roughly corresponds with the time he was film critic, include *England Made Me* (1935), *A Gun for Sale* (1936), *Brighton Rock* (1938), and *The Confidential Agent* (1939). This grouping may be stretched further into the war years to include *The Power and the Glory*

(1940) and *The Ministry of Fear* (1943), though *The Power and the Glory* is better placed with the Catholic problem novels that were written during and just after the war.

The first three published novels, which most critics would include in the list of Greene's early social books, do not really belong there. Their themes are unlike those of the social novels he wrote while he was film critic, and their style is different. They are, as Greene himself admits, "of a badness beyond the power of criticism properly to evoke—the prose [is] flat and stilted and in the case of *Rumour at Nightfall* pretentious, . . . the characterization non-existent."[77] There is "terrible misuse of simile and metaphor."[78] "There are far too many adjectives and too much explanation of motive, no trust in the reader's understanding, and overlong description."[79] All these problems, which Greene mentions in *Ways of Escape*, might be attributed to the inexperience of an apprentice. But there are more interesting ineptitudes. The crosscutting from scene to scene, which Greene later developed to perfection, is not incisive here. The use of visual detail to create character and atmosphere, which we recognize as one of Greene's artistic signatures, is inconspicuous. The presentation of action is imprecise, and the dialogue, which is so much a part of action in a novel, is cumbersome and cluttered with long passages of morbid introspection.

It is for the mastery of precisely these problems that Greene has come to be called a "cinematic" novelist. When we compare a few passages from novels written in the second half of the 1930s with some from the earlier novels, we see that the "visual" quality associated with Greene's style becomes pronounced during the time he watched those four hundred films as critic for the *Spectator*.

In *Brighton Rock*, Spicer hurries away from Pinkie's house:

He didn't even wait to fetch his hat. His hair was thin on top, dry and brittle over the dandruff. He walked rapidly, going nowhere in particular, but every road in Brighton ended on the front. . . . he wanted to be alone, he went down the stone steps to the level of the beach; it was early closing and the small shops facing the sea under the promenade were closed. He walked on the edge of the asphalt, scuffling in the shingle. I wouldn't grass, he remarked dumbly to the tide as it lifted and withdrew, but it wasn't my doing, I never wanted to kill Fred. He passed into shadow under the pier, and a cheap photographer with a box camera snapped him as the shadow fell and pressed a paper into his hand. Spicer didn't notice. The iron pillars stetched down across the wet dimmed

shingle holding up above his head the motor-track, the shooting booths
and peep machines, mechanical models, "the Robot Man will tell your
fortune." A seagull flew straight towards him between the pillars like a
scared bird caught in a cathedral, then swerved out into the sunlight
from the dark iron nave. I wouldn't grass, Spicer said, unless I had to. . . .
He stumbled on an old boot and put his hand on the stones to save
himself: they had all the cold of the sea and had never been warmed by sun
under these pillars.[80]

Greene's use of visual detail to evoke circumstance is masterful.
Compare Spicer's walk with Francis Andrews's in the earlier book *The
Man Within*:

> He reached the downs as a first orange glow lifted above the eastern
> horizon. Its fragile soaring beauty, like a butterfly with delicate pow-
> dered wings resting on a silver leaf, touched him and increased his
> shame. . . .
>
> From where he walked it was not yet light enough to see the valley
> clearly. Only at intervals the red spark of a lighted window would make a
> crevice in the gray veil, and after he had walked some miles a cock crew.
> The downs were bare of life save for the occasional brooding hunched
> form of a dark tree. He walked, and as he walked the first poignancy of his
> shame departed and the events of the night slipped a little way into
> shadow. When Andrews realized this he stayed for a moment still and
> strove to drag them back. For this had happened many times before. It
> was the first stage toward a repetition of the sin, this forgetfulness. How
> could he ever keep clean if the sense of shame was so short-lived? "After
> all, I enjoyed myself," he thought against his will, "why repent? It's a
> coward's part. Go back and do it again. Why run my head into danger?"
> With an effort he clenched his will and ran, to stifle thought, ran fast
> until he had no more breath and flung himself down upon the grass.[81]

How imprecise this earlier passage is in its use of detail. Here the
setting is but a backdrop for Francis's reverie. In the *Brighton Rock*
passage the detail of place is woven together with character in such a
way that Spicer's situation cannot be separated from his ambience.

When Pinkie meets Colleoni at the Cosmopolitan in *Brighton Rock*,
Greene uses the same cinematic precision of detail to make Colleoni
appear larger than life to the seventeen-year-old gangster and to
create the abyss between the two men that gives their meeting such
irony. But in *Rumour at Nightfall* Greene has trouble convincing us of
Caveda's equally large stature with his fuzzy description:

"He is a much abused man. He is a Liberal. Oh, yes, he calls himself a Carlist, but what does he care for such politics? The caballero knows what a dirty game they are. Caveda is not a politician. He cares for the great, the fundamental things, Liberalism, the poor, freedom. He does not believe in priests. Kings, what are they beside the people? . . .
He calls himself a Carlist, yes. But a man must have a banner. It is . . . respectable."[82]

In that novel changes of time and scene are handled slowly. There are no rapid montage cuts as in the later books:

. . . back in London, where a man could see quite a long way in front of him.[83]

Closing the door softly he strayed into the passage.[84]

Everything is seen here, every move told. Compare this with *Brighton Rock*, where even in one paragraph, like Pinkie's story of Annie Collins, Greene crosscuts without hesitation backward and forward through time:

"She went to the same school I did," the Boy said. He took a look down the grey street and then the glass before *Married Passion* reflected again his young and hopeless face. "She put her head on the line," he said, "up by Hassocks. She had to wait ten minutes for the seven-five. Fog made it late from Victoria. Cut off her head. She was fifteen. She was going to have a baby and she knew what it was like. She'd had one two years before, and they could 'ave pinned it on twelve boys."[85]

How much of chronological time Greene has deleted from his writing. There is no commentary here, no interpretation, as there would have been in the earlier novels. There is only an extraordinarily terse presentation of facts. The fog, the late train, the ten-minute wait for death. No commentary could say more of Annie's determination and despair; in fact, any would weaken the scene. Here Greene conceals in order to strengthen the image; he employs speech as he suggested it should be used in film, to counterpoint the visual. Because the visible stands alone, the reader experiences Annie's death very much as he would if he saw it on film, without intellectual interpretation. His concentration is simply shifted for a paragraph from the present to the past, from the wider picture of Pinkie to the close-up of a memory recalled from another point of view, objectively, as though a camera had shot it. And the scene sinks into the story

as a shot would into a film—one image, one change of focus from the
foreground to the background of Pinkie's character. Then the focus is
readjusted. The conversation between Pinkie and Dallow continues,
making no reference to the story of Annie Collins. There is an ellipsis.
What does Pinkie think about Annie? What did Annie think while
she waited on the track? We are told nothing more than a camera
would show us and are left to reconstruct the importance of the scene
for ourselves.

Perhaps the best way to see the development of these "visual"
qualities in Greene's style is to look at similar sequences from several
novels written during the period in question. If we examine the love
scenes in *The Man Within* and *The Name of Action*, we see that they are
composed of long drawn out descriptions of action interwoven with
interior monologue and dialogue connected by lengthy anecdotal
phrases. One such scene in *The Man Within* begins with Andrews
addressing a star with words meant for Elizabeth: " 'After all,' he said
to the star, 'I shall never see you again, and must I therefore never
know another woman? I cannot come to you, for they will be
watching for me there, and you do not love me.' " The scene ends
about ten pages later, after he has made love to another woman,
thinking all the while that "he was raising a barrier of time between
Elizabeth and any help which he might bring. . . . he could not forget
the dream, vision, fantasy, what you will, which he had seen in the
candle's light."[86]

The same indecisiveness and lengthy introspection takes up much
of similar scenes in *The Name of Action*. When Oliver Chant and
Anne-Marie Demassener, whom he loves, finally find themselves
alone in a gasthaus, they hum and ha for several pages before
Anne-Marie tells Chant to "turn out the light."[87]

In *Stamboul Train* things are different. Coral's loss of virginity
occupies about four pages. There is more visual detail here— Coral
undresses "slowly and very methodically, folding each garment in
turn, the blouse, the skirt, the bodice, the vest, and laying it in a neat
pile on the opposite seat"—and tighter dialogue. But most of the
action is still concealed in thought:

> The sense of unfamiliarity deepened round him. It was as if he had
> started out from home on a familiar walk, past the gas works, across the
> brick bridge over the Wimble, across two fields, and found himself not
> in the lane which ran uphill to the new road and the bungalows, but on

the threshold of a strange wood, faced by a shaded path he had never taken, running God knows where. . . . He had never before felt lust rising in him and yet checked and increasing because of the check.

. . . Her laughter lay, an almost imperceptible pool of sound, beneath the pounding and the clatter of the express.

The sense of strangeness survived even the customary gestures; lying in the berth she proved awkward in a mysterious innocent fashion which astonished him. Her laughter stopped, not coming gradually to an end, but vanishing so that he wondered whether he had imagined the sound or whether it had been a trick of the glancing wheels.[88]

By *It's a Battlefield* things have changed considerably. Discussion between Conrad and Milly is short:

"Listen," he said quietly, "you know I love you. Let me stay. That was why I came upstairs. I couldn't sleep." He felt no guilt at all; this did not harm his brother, this hopeless attempt to shield her, for she had not even been deceived; she was glad, she was grateful, she was his friend, but she didn't believe a word he said. Then she touched him with timidity, and his flesh stirred, and he felt a degree of guilt which only the bed and the tiring of his body and the forgetting of his love in the direct contact of skin with skin, the thrust of lust, could temporarily and in part assuage. When he felt her shudder, he had a dull sense of an irrevocable injury which one of them had done to the other. Love had been close to him, in the kitchen, before the glow and the hum of the gas, between chair and chair, which had escaped him now in the bed, in the dark. One of them had injured the other, but it was not their fault. They had been driven to it, and holding her body close to him with painful tenderness, it was hate he chiefly felt, hate of Jim, of a director's nephew, of two men laughing in Picadilly. When he awoke in the night she was crying, and nothing that he could do would stop her tears. He thought of Kay happily asleep in the next room and lust, he thought, they call that lust and this love. He meant the hate and the pain and the sense of guilt and the sound of crying in the greying room and sleeplessness and the walls shaking as the early morning lorries drove out of London.[89]

There is still analysis of the scene through interior monologue, still deliberation on action. But what is visible begins to stand on its own, and Greene reinforces it by connecting it to "the greying room" and the "early morning lorries."

In *Brighton Rock* the presentation is far more restrained:

"Me?" He laughed at her unconvincingly and advanced: an embryo of sensuality—he was mocked by the memory of a gown, a back, "I loved you that first time in Santa Monica. . ." Shaken by a kind of rage, he took her by the shoulders. He had escaped from Nelson Place to this: he pushed her against the bed. "It's mortal sin," he said, getting what savour there was out of innocence, trying to taste God in the mouth: a brass bedball, her dumb, frightened and acquiescent eyes—he blotted everything out in a sad brutal now-or-never embrace: a cry of pain and then the jangling of the bell beginning all over again. "Christ," he said, "can't they let a man alone?" He opened his eyes on the grey room to see what he had done: it seemed to him more like death than when Hale and Spicer had died.[90]

We have waited two hundred pages for this scene. It takes one paragraph. The events are described almost totally from the outside, and in what very little introspection there is, Greene uses visual detail—"the memory of a gown," "Nelson Place"—to link action with the psychological, sociological, and religious. We see the scene through Pinkie's eyes—"a brass bedball, her dumb, frightened and acquiescent eyes"—and then, as Pinkie "blotted everything out," Greene changes focus with "the jangling of the bell." Here is a picture of behavior or action, not of the reasons for it.

This is not to say that action was not important in Greene's writing before. It always was. But Greene seemed incapable of allowing it to stand on its own before. Here there is an understanding that action, or the visible, public part of a character, can almost tell the tale alone. This kind of objective honesty is difficult to find in the novels of the early thirties.

Looking over these passages, one sees the metamorphosis in Greene's style. It came, he says, with *Stamboul Train*:

That year, 1931, for the first and last time in my life I deliberately set out to write a book to please, one which with luck might be made into a film. . . . I suppose the popular success of . . . *Grand Hotel* gave me the idea of how to set about winning the jackpot. . . . In those days I thought in terms of a key scene—I would even chart its position on a sheet of paper before I began to write. . . . Often these scenes consisted of isolating two characters—hiding in a railway shed in *Stamboul Train*, in an empty house in *A Gun For Sale*. It was as though I wanted to escape from the vast liquidity of the novel and to play out the most important situation on a narrow stage where I could direct every movement of my characters. A scene like that halts the progress of the novel with dramatic emphasis, just as in a film a close-up makes the moving picture momentarily pause.[91]

Clearly the style has changed. In *Stamboul Train* the dialogue is more dramatic than it is in the first three novels, the detail more profuse, and the action more suspenseful. As well, with the change of genre from historical romance to thriller and of setting from the past to the present the earlier introspective vagueness is greatly reduced. As many critics have pointed out, it is here that Greene's writing begins to come into focus, and it is interesting that he took his direction from the film. But the very tight cutting, the flat observation of events made almost exclusively from the outside, the behaviorist view of character, the concealing of facts in significant detail—these techniques that mark Greene's mature style are undeveloped in *Stamboul Train*. Indeed, in his next novel, *It's a Battlefield* (1934), many of the problems of the first three books reappear.

In the years between *Stamboul Train* and *It's a Battlefield*, Greene was intensely preoccupied with his novelist's craft. He became excited by the work of Henry James and Ford Madox Ford and by Percy Lubbock's *The Craft of Fiction*. In the literary reviews he wrote for the *Spectator* just before he became film critic, he discussed his earlier interest in Jacobean drama and explored the problems of writing melodrama. When he began reviewing films, he continued this discussion and also considered the advantages film had in handling melodramatic material.

In 1935 he wrote that the stage has to transform melodramatic material by depth of characterization or by placing the individual drama in its general setting. "The camera, because it can note with more exactitude and vividness than the prose of most living playwrights the atmosphere of mean streets and cheap lodgings, gives the story background and authenticity."[92] The violence is explained and therefore ceases to be melodramatic. By the end of the 1930s, Greene had learned to transform melodrama superbly in his own novels, but in the middle of the decade, and despite the changes of style made in *Stamboul Train*, we find him still searching for better methods.

It would be suppositious to say that the steady viewing of films between 1935 and 1940 changed the way he wrote. In 1974, Greene thought it did not. "*It's a Battlefield*," he told Gene Phillips, "is the only one of my novels that was intentionally based on film techniques and it was written in 1934, before I had done any film scripts. It was my only deliberate attempt to tell a story in cinematic terms."[93] But sources of influence are often difficult to attribute, and in 1980, in

Ways of Escape, Greene acknowledged finding cinematic direction for other novels. *Stamboul Train* was influenced by *Grand Hotel* and *A Gun for Sale* benefited from cinematic-like key scenes, a technique Greene continued to use as late as *The Comedians* (1966). Yet even these more recent disclosures fail to consider the years of film criticism and the possible effect of *watching* stories on the way one perceives.

From *Stamboul Train* on, Greene was trying new fictional methods, partly in an attempt to produce a financially successful book. The cinema, he says, showed him some of the more obvious techniques that he adopted. Did it not also influence some of the finer changes in his style? It is clear that he brought a literary slant to his cinema reviews; it should be no surprise that he carried to his fiction a cinematic flavor from the four hundred films he had watched.

In the years to come, the narrative pattern and structure of his novels changed. There is a shift in the point of view from which the stories are told. Before 1950 the narrator is always omniscient, but thereafter half the novels are written in the first person. There is a change in the class backgrounds of the characters from lower to middle class. And there are the corresponding philosophical changes that enable us to divide the fiction into three groups: the early social novels written before and during the war; the Catholic problem novels that appear during and just after the war; and the comico-political novels that comprise the bulk of his work after 1950. Yet throughout, Greene's style continues to be distinguished by the "cinematic" technques he perfected during his years as film reviewer.

If it is difficult to pinpoint the exact effect of these years on Greene's novels, it is easy to assess the film criticism itself. One has only to choose at random from the many reviews and articles to be entertained by a witty and creative journalist and to see that although Greene sometimes reviewed as many as four films a week, he found space in his columns for far more than outlining plots and suggesting entertainment.

His ideas about a common and poetic cinema were not unique: what he sought in the commonplace was similar to what Grierson looked for. Both desired to make a drama from the ordinary. Both desired that the camera dig deeply into everyday life, capturing the things that most often went unnoticed. What Greene described as contrasting poetic images was similar, although greatly simplified, to Eisenstein's concept of montage, or to what he called in *Film Form* "montage trope," which created "a new quality of the whole from a juxtaposition of the separate parts."[94] Greene's desire to create for an audience what *it* wanted was similar to what Charlie Chaplin in fact did. It was the combination of these ideas that was fresh, and, flowing from Greene's incisive pen, it quickly gained him a reputation as "the best film critic we had."[95]

The combination came not from a film background but from a literary one, and it is heavily weighted with the artistic concerns he shared with other writers during the thirties. "Poetry," Auden wrote in 1935, "is not concerned with telling people what to do, but with extending our knowledge of good and evil, perhaps making the necessity for action more urgent and its nature more clear, but only leading us to the point where it is possible for us to make a rational and moral choice."[96]

Bracketed by two wars, the writers of Greene's generation were all, in a broad sense, intensely political writers. Their art was molded by the "fantastic realities" of a world they knew had to be changed. As individuals they responded differently, but as a generation of writers they shared a moral commitment to use their pens to alert men to the need for action. Although Greene was neither a film theoretician nor a writer primarily interested in film, he saw clearly that if directors used film honestly and with a sense of social purpose the millions of apathetic viewers who went weekly to the movies not to see something in particular but to see anything that happened to be on the screen could be made to consider rationally the realities of their world.

In calling for a popular and poetic cinema, Greene called for artists to be responsible to their craft and to their audience. Film, he believed, should be an art—it should contain individual artistic vision—but it should also perform a social role, which was "to suggest human values."[97]

2

First
Confrontations

"From film reviewing it was only a small step to scriptwriting,"
wrote Greene, who took that step in 1937 when he met Alexander
Korda. He had "persistently attacked the films made by . . . Korda,"
and perhaps, he thought, Korda

> became curious to meet his enemy. He asked my agent to bring me to
> Denham Film Studios and when we were alone he asked if I had any film
> story in mind. I had none, so I began to improvise a thriller—early
> morning on Platform 1 at Paddington, the platform empty, except for
> one man who is waiting for the last train from Wales. From below his
> raincoat a trickle of blood forms a pool on the platform.[1]

For the next two months Greene was paid what he then considered
the "extravagant salary" of £60 a week to write *The Green Cockatoo*.[2]

The film is about a girl from the West Country (played by Rene
Ray), who travels alone by train to London. En route she is told by
another passenger that someone at Whitehall 1212 will help her in

the city if she telephones when she arrives. At the phone booth she
meets Dave Connor (Robert Newton), who, dying from stab wounds
inflicted by racetrack gangsters he has doublecrossed, is trying to
make contact with his brother Jim (John Mills). Eileen takes him to a
hotel, where he dies mumbling, "Find Jim Connor at the Green
Cockatoo." She flees the scene after the landlady finds her holding a
dagger she has pulled from Dave's side, and the story tells of her
flight through Soho in search of the Green Cockatoo. Jim, it turns
out, is a singer and dancer there. He distrusts Eileen because she has
been followed by Terrell (Charles Oliver), the leader of the racetrack
gang. Terrell is eventually arrested, and Eileen marries Jim.

Greene considered *The Green Cockatoo*, which was not released until
1940, "the worse and least successful of Korda's productions,"[3] most
of which he continued to pan in his reviews. But the fault was not
Greene's; E. O. Berkman had written the script; William Cameron
Menzies had directed it. So this first venture into screenwriting left
him professionally unscathed, if personally disquieted by what had
happened to his story during the cinematic process. The film, in fact,
not only began his lifelong flirtation with moviemaking but gained
him Korda's friendship, "which endured and deepened till . . .
[Korda's] death."[4]

Although *The Green Cockatoo* was the first narrative Greene created
for the cinema, it was not his first story to be screened. In 1932, soon
before he began work as a film critic, he had sold *Stamboul Train* to
Twentieth Century-Fox for £1,500. Somewhat embarrassed by the
film, he later wrote: "I was down to £30 in the bank, a child on the
way; I had been refused the job of sub-editor on the *Catholic Herald*
because my qualifications were held to be 'too good,' and I had no
prospects. . . . It enabled me to go on writing without seeking other
employment."[5] In *Journey Without Maps* he described the picture
(renamed *Orient Express* and released in 1933) as "cheap, . . . the
direction was incompetent, the photography undistinguished, the
story sentimental. If there was any truth in the original it had been
carefully altered, if anything was left unchanged it was because it was
untrue."[6]

As he reported in *International Film Annual*, "a second prize came
my way in 1934, when Paramount bought *A Gun For Sale* for . . .
£2500."[7] The film appeared in 1942 as *This Gun for Hire*. In it
Veronica Lake and Robert Preston played opposite a newcomer to the

screen, Alan Ladd, who, as Raven, hid a crippled wrist in his coat pocket. The wrist was an unfortunate substitute for the original Raven's harelip, because it drastically reduced the hero's psychological complexity. And there were more ticklish changes. The setting was moved from England in the 1930s to California in the 1940s. To update the story for American audiences, the film had fifth columnists selling documents to the Japanese, and Ellen Graham (Anne in the novel) was turned into an FBI agent. Yet despite these broad departures from Greene's story, most of the novel's excitement survived. And oddly, given the changes in setting, the book's cold, violent atmosphere was faithfully reproduced.

A second adaptation of the novel, directed by James Cagney and entitled *Short Cut to Hell*, was made in 1957. This film was based on W. R. Burnett's earlier script for *This Gun for Hire* and, like its predecessor, was released by Paramount. Here Robert Ivers played Raven (renamed Kyle), and Georgann Johnson played Anne (now called Glory). The setting was Oakland, California. Kyle was hired to kill a city engineer, Carl Adams, who had discovered that faulty steel caused the collapse of a building under construction. Like *This Gun for Hire*, the film was exciting and incorporated Greene's theme of betrayal, but it too lacked the psychological complexity of the novel.

Looking back on the sale of these two books, Greene wrote: "my first feeling towards the film is one of gratitude. . . . You take the money, you can go on writing for another year or two, you have no just ground of complaint." After all, "when you sell a book to Hollywood you sell it outright. The long Hollywood contracts— sheet after closely printed sheet as long as the first treatment of the novel which is for sale—ensure that you have no 'author's rights.' The film producer can alter anything."[8]

Yet having taken the money so that he could survive "a little above the lean," he found it difficult to forget the inconsequential adaptations of his work that followed. "The . . . chance of winning a kind of Irish sweep, of receiving money for the outright sale of work already done,"[9] conflicted with his expectations for the cinema. And he soon learned that having novels twisted beyond recognition was not the worst affront he would suffer in working for the film business.

In 1940, when his adaptation of John Galsworthy's *The First and the Last* was released under the title *Twenty-one Days*, he discovered that "film-making can be a pretty distressing business for, when all is said and done, a writer's part . . . is relatively small."[10] It was an unfortunate early script for Greene. In his *Spectator* review of the film he explained that the play "was peculiarly unsuited for film adaptation, as its whole point lay in a double suicide (forbidden by the censor), a burned confession, and an innocent man's conviction for murder (forbidden by the great public)."[11] Later he added that "if the story had any force at all it lay in its extreme sensationalism, but as the sensation was impossible under the rules, . . . there was little of Galsworthy's plot left when I had finished."[12]

Galsworthy's story told of the suicides of Larry Durrant and Wanda Wallen, suicides preceded by the murder of Wanda's husband, the conviction of an innocent man, and the inability of Larry, the real murderer, to confess without tarnishing the reputation of his brother Keith, a lawyer about to be made a judge. Wanda and Larry died in each other's arms, having left a note in which they asked to be buried together. To avoid any connection between himself and the earlier murder, Keith destroyed the letter, clearing the way for his appointment as judge.

The film showed Keith to be corrupt, as did Galsworthy's play; it pointed a finger at the British system of justice; and it revealed Larry's confusion about confessing to the murder. But it also had the innocent man die en route to jail, which spared Larry his confession and enabled Keith to save face. These changes dissolved the visual disparity Galsworthy had created between the lovers' laughter as they took the pills (Wanda dressed in her bridal gown) and the irrevocability of what they were doing and destroyed the contrast between the lovers' simple honesty and "Keith's world—all righteous will-power and success."[13] Since, as Greene believed, these elements were poetic and central to the story, he had reason to blame the film's failure on "the rules of the British Board of Film Censors, who forbade suicide and forbade a failure of English justice."[14]

And not only the censors meddled with *Twenty-one Days*. In the *Spectator*, Greene indicated there was a suicide in the original script, "the only suicide the censorship allowed." This, he discovered "with some astonishment" when he saw the film, was "cut out."[15] Its omission added to the picture's failure, and he believes that Vivien Leigh (Wanda) and Laurence Olivier (Larry) were also to blame, thought he says as well that they had much to forgive him. They went "off for a weekend of love," delaying the shooting of the ending and breaking the concentration of the actors and crew. When they returned in the "wrong spirit," Greene felt that whatever atmosphere the film had had was ruined.[16] Even "the brilliant acting of Mr. Hay Petrie as a decayed and outcast curate" could not prevent the picture from being "slow, wordy, unbearably sentimental." Greene emerged from the experience "swearing never, never to do it again."[17]

Within a year he was to provide the commentary for *The New Britain*, a documentary made by Paul Rotha's company, Strand Films. In 1937 he had helped Rotha with the narration for an earlier Strand Films documentary, the highly successful *The Future's in the Air*. That movie had been directed by Alexander Shaw and produced and edited by Paul Rotha and was one of three the unit made under contract with Imperial Airways. It was intended to celebrate the inauguration of the Empire Air Mail and was shown as a second feature in commercial cinemas, running for sixteen weeks in London's West End alone.

The film opens on an isolated airstrip in the outback of Australia. The date is January, 1937, the weather dazzling hot, the sound track silent. In the second sequence the silence is interrupted by the drone of an airplane, which comes into focus and lands. A man carrying letters walks to a shed, and the commentary begins. From here the film takes its viewers over mountains and rivers on a journey eastward. The superb shots of bazaars and temples, of women working on Karachi building sites, of Angkor Wat, are interwoven with the commentary and William Alwyn's music, which becomes more exotic as the film moves farther east. The result is a magnificent and highly successful travelogue.

The New Britain (1940) was a different kind of documentary. It was a propaganda short showing Britain's accomplishments between the two world wars, directed by Ralph Keene and produced by Alexander Shaw. Its effect lay entirely in Greene's commentary, which builds into a litany of the country's social achievements since 1918. The film begins with fast cuts of World War I soldiers fighting and marching. The narrator comments, "Then we turned to build a new Britain." Shops, factories, and universities flash across the screen: the building of bridges, docks, and roads. Greene adds: "We didn't think those lights would ever go out." We watch children playing, going to school, bicycling; adults going to the cinema, coming from the library, drinking in pubs. Greene interpolates: "We forgot Jerry."

At first the idea appears effective. Greene's "We forgot Jerry" is a poignant reminder of the difference between a pacific prewar Britain and a Britain engaged in a struggle for her life. But the antithesis quickly loses its bite when he begins to sound like a referee at an increasingly melodramatic match between "Jerry" and the British, "the ordinary people for whom all these things were done." Even in a wartime propaganda film it is difficult to forget the depression, the general strike, and mass unemployment and to accept such a utopian image of Britain as Greene's commentary suggests: "There was light and cleanliness. . . . In the factories employer and employee worked together for the common good. . . . One million exchanged slum for sun, . . . a world of love, peace and security, . . . with a coastline simple, unboastful and unbreakable."

Today the film seems a mechanical attempt to create popular poetic cinema. The elements are there: the pictures of ordinary people engaged in ordinary occupations, the mass feeling, the critical contrast. But the commentary is too predictable. There is no uncertainty, no ambiguity, no surprise. The images form a redundant series of consecutive juxtapositions rather than create new impressions.

Greene's second cinematic contribution to the war effort was more interesting and far more effective. *Went the Day Well?* directed by Alberto Cavalcanti and released from Ealing Studios in 1942, was adapted by John Dighton, Diana Morgan, and Angus MacPhail from Greene's story "The Lieutenant Died Last." The film begins, as does the later *Third Man*, with a narrator remembering a series of incidents. "Good day to you," he says, as he stands in a small country cemetery smoking his pipe. "It will be this—the names on the graves that brought you." The camera moves in for a close shot of German names on the tombstones. In the background is the local church; the amens of a boys' choir drift through its open doors.

The film shows an invasion of Britain by Germans who, disguised as Royal Engineers on maneuvers, occupy the small town of Bramley End with the help of the local squire (Leslie Banks). A series of bunglings—a crossed number 7 on a game score, a discarded chocolate wrapper marked "Chokolade Wien"—leads the villagers to discover the soldiers' identity. The village children are subsequently locked in the manor house and the adults in the church. Several escapes are attempted, and a boy finally gets through to a neighboring village to summon the British army. This occurs, however, only after several villagers have been killed recapturing their town and the traitor squire has been shot by Nora (Valerie Taylor), whom he was to have married on May 24, 1942, the day the invasion began.

Greene's original story was rather different. In it the Germans, in uniform, parachute into Potter and round up the villagers, whom they promise not to harm unless someone tries to escape. Old Bill Purves has gone unnoticed. He is the local poacher who disappears three or four times a year with a bottle of whisky to drink, sleep, and hunt on Lord Drew's estate. On the day of the story Purves is on one of his escapades. He sees the Germans shoot young Brewitt "humanely, at the legs." Fortified with whisky, with the Boer War in mind and his forty-year-old Mauser in hand, he kills the invaders. Last to die is the lieutenant in whose pocket Purves finds a photo of a naked baby on a hearthrug. For years to come he will tell any villager who listens the story of that day, always omitting the part about the lieutenant. Whenever he looked at the picture, "it made him—for no reason that *he* could understand—feel bad."[18]

Although the focus of Greene's story was changed to allow the somewhat broader perspective necessary in a popular propaganda film, Cavalcanti paid great attention to the fabric of the local setting in the original. By 1942 he was well known in England for his work with the General Post Office Unit, or the Crown Film Unit as it was known by then, which he had joined in the early thirties, and *Went the Day Well?* clearly benefited from his documentarist's respect for the minutiae of realistic detail. In his review of the film James Agee, himself a novelist, film critic, and screenwriter, called the picture "remarkably lifelike."[19] The small girl bringing a cup of tea to her wounded father, the children at breakfast, the poacher meeting the young boy in the muddy woods—the attention to particulars in these and other scenes gave both the characters and the situation plausibility and turned Greene's already suspenseful story into a very effective propaganda thriller. The film understandably had great appeal to wartime British audiences, the more so since it was set at a later date, after a successful end to the war, and it was popular in the United States as well, under the title *48 Hours*.

The New Britain and *Went the Day Well?* were the last of his films with which Greene was closely associated until 1947 when *Brighton Rock*, for which he wrote the script, was released. In the interim, he sold himself "to MGM on a slave contract under which they owned everything I did," he says. "When the war was over and I left government service, I wasn't confident of being able to support the family on writing. I had done very little writing during the war." One of the results of his "slavery" to Metro-Goldwyn-Mayer is a film treatment entitled *The Tenth Man*,[20] the manuscript of which is housed in the Humanities Research Center at the University of Texas, Austin.

The story is set in France immediately after its liberation in 1944. It is about a group of imprisoned men who are forced to choose from among themselves three who will be shot. They draw lots. One of the three who draws a marked paper is Louis Cheval, a wealthy lawyer. He pays a poor man everything he has to take his place. When Cheval is released from prison he takes the name Jean-Louis Charlot and returns to his old house, which is now owned by the dead man's family. An intrigue ensues about his identity. The story is complicated by his falling in love with the dead man's sister, the appearance of another man using the same name, and antagonism between people who collaborated with the Germans during the occupation and those who resisted.

Between *Went the Day Well?* and *Brighton Rock* four more novels were turned into films, but Greene took no part in their adaptation. *Ministry of Fear*, released in 1944, was the first of these. Although Fritz Lang, its director, was able to capture some of the atmosphere of the novel (at the fair and in the tube station during the blackout), the film lacked the psychological depth of Greene's work. The journey into fear through which Greene leads Arthur Rowe, confused about his reasons for killing his already dying wife, is played down in the film (where Rowe is called Stephen Neale, played by Ray Milland), while the wartime intrigue in the story is brought into prominence. The result is a fast-moving spy story, something of a propaganda thriller, but nothing like Greene's novel, in which Rowe's moral dilemma becomes the psychological analogue of man caught in the nightmare of war. Because in the film Stephen Neale does not kill his wife—she takes the poison he has bought and hidden in a drawer while he debates whether or not to give it to her—a good deal of Greene's story becomes senseless. Presumably that is why the scenes in the mental clinic were not included in the film. Greene thought them "the best in the novel," and was surprised "that Fritz Lang, the old director of *M.* and *The Spy*, omitted them altogether, . . . thus making the whole story meaningless."[21]

In explanation Fritz Lang has said that he originally agreed to do the film because "I admired the author, Graham Greene, very much . . . but when . . . I saw what had been done with the script, [by Seton I. Miller] I was terribly shocked and I said, 'I want to get out of this contract.' The agent said I couldn't. . . . I had signed a contract and I had to fulfill it, that's all."[22]

The second film, *Confidential Agent*, was released by Warner Brothers two years later, in 1945. Of the American adaptations this has continued to be Greene's favorite. In fact, it is the only one he has ever said he "quite liked." He commented that the screenplay by Robert Buckner "followed the book closely," and that "Lauren Bacall [Rose Cullen] and Charles Boyer [Denard, in the novel, D.] were exceptionally good."[23] The film was certainly, to that date, the best attempt to put Greene's work on the screen. Yet it was still not entirely successful. The settings and atmospheres, which by this time had stamped Greene's novels as "cinematic," were not entirely realized. Agee commented that "this is odd, because . . . Greene achieves in print what more naturally belonged in films, and in a sense does not write novels at all, but verbal movies."[24]

Charles Dickens once remarked to George Henry Lewes "that every word said by his characters was distinctly *heard* by him."[25] Perhaps Greene's experience with the blank page is the modern analogue: when he writes he "watches" his characters, and his eyes get extremely tired in the process.[26] He begins, as in *The Green Cockatoo*, not so much with an idea as with a mood: "*The Heart of The Matter* started with one character seeing another character pass in the street, and one didn't fully know what was going to happen to these characters. There was a mood of heat, of tiredness, of injustice."[27]

For Greene, writing is visual encounter with a place, a tone, a person. The characters are fluid. As his eye roams about a setting picking a detail here, pointing at something there, they take on verbal shape and become fixed not only with their visible individual peculiarities but with the intricate detail of the background in which they were visualized. For this reason Pinkie without Brighton, circa 1935, would not be Pinkie and the whisky priest without Mexico in the midst of the Christero movement not the whisky priest. Visual detail, or what has been labeled "atmosphere," actually describes character. Take, for example, a sketch of the manageress at D.'s hotel in *The Confidential Agent:*

> It was a bully's face; she should have been a man, with that square jaw, the shady determination, the impetigo. . . . He looked curiously round at the den—that was the best word for it. It wasn't a woman's room at all, with its square unclothed table, its leather chairs, no flowers, no frippery, a cupboard for shoes. It seemed made and furnished for nothing but use. The cupboard door was open full of heavy, low-heeled, sensible shoes.[28]

The description is heavily weighted with perceptual information. The style is not analytical; the manageress does not evolve from lengthy analysis or intellectual discussion. She is flatly and directly presented through the accumulation of detail that Greene's camera eye records. In its particulars the sketch seems visual, and what is more, because the manageress is fixed permanently against a set, it seems to form a unit of action similar to a cinematic sequence.

As Richard Hoggart observed thirty years ago in his essay "The Force of Caricature," the visual in Greene's writing is so persistent that the very structure of his sentences is affected by it. In using the simile, he often reverses the usual order of comparison—abstract to concrete—and begins with the concrete. The whisky priest "drank brandy down like damnation";[29] "Dr. Bellows moved here and there erratically like love."[30] He frequently adds a visual quality to his characters' feelings through personification: "loneliness," we are told, "moved along the crowded pavement"[31] at Martins's side. "Cruelty grew at the sight"[32] of Baines, and "justice waited behind a wooden counter on a high stool"[33] for Philip.

At first glance this style seems easily filmable because it is so dependent of perceptual information, but the connection between Greene's characters and the objects around them is neither simple nor merely visual. It points to the relationship in his novels between people and society. Here society generates and controls its members. Settings are never two-dimensional; they are active forces—physical representations of the moral worlds that have produced the characters. Action does not occur against the settings; it happens because of them.

The method gives Greene enormous structural advantage as a novelist but harbors a trap for the film maker. In the lines "My Luve is like a red, red rose, / That's newly sprung in June," Burns uses the simile to give love concreteness. With her customary sensitivity Virginia Woolf noted that he "presents us with impressions of moisture and warmth and the flow of crimson and the softness of petals inextricably mixed and strung upon the life of a rhythm which is itself the voice of passion and the hesitation of the love."[34] When Greene writes "The world was all steel and gold, like war,"[35] and "The water lapped like doubt,"[36] he is doing the reverse. He is abstracting the concrete. The images are immensely effective, but they are neither as visual nor as specific as Burns's.

Greene does a similar thing on a larger scale with his characters. He breathes life into them by making abstract the trappings of their environment. In this way, even more than in his cataloguing, he links the animate and inanimate, a conjunction that seems cinematic but is next to impossible to film. In *The Confidential Agent* he tells us D. "carried the war with him. Wherever D. was, there was the war. . . . He began to tramp—up and down beside the rail—to keep warm, his head down, the deck like a map marked with trenches, impossible positions, salients, deaths: bombing planes took flight from between his eyes, and in his brain the mountains shook with shell-bursts."[37] D.'s state of mind is made "visible" through a simile that extends to include not only the train platform but himself as part of the battlefield.

How could this be adapted to film? If we look back at the metamorphosis that took place in Greene's style during the second half of the thirties, we see that, as this description of D.'s disease would be difficult to put on the screen, so would many of the "cinematic" passages cited. The account of Andrews's feelings as he walked across the downs in *The Man Within* was sentimental and imprecise in contrast to that of Spicer's state of mind as he approached the edge of the asphalt on Brighton beach, but it is much easier to capture on film "the occasional brooding hunched form" against "the first glow" than to show the meaning of Spicer's stumbling on the old boot and the coldness under his hands of the stones that "had never been warmed by sun." Whereas the earlier novel was full of endless explorations of motive, long descriptions, and fuzzy metaphors that made it sentimental and verbally imprecise, its plot was coherent and exciting and might have been put to good cinematic use. Spicer's situation is verbally clear because Greene binds his state of mind to the visual detail of setting, but it would be difficult to film because of this very conjunction of the empirical and the psychological.

Paradoxically, as Greene's writing became increasingly "cinematic" during the thirties, it may also have become more difficult to adapt. He mastered the employment of empirical reality to signify the mental continuum, and this gave his writing tremendous precision, but how could this process be transferred to celluloid? Film uses concrete objects to make the spectator imagine and remember; it does not use them the way Greene does, as a substitute for thought. His style appeared "visual" because of the way he employed crosscutting and ellipsis and linked physical detail to character development, dialogue to action, but at least here, in *The Confidential Agent*, it proved stubbornly verbal in adaptation. This is no doubt why Agee closed his review of the film with the remark that Greene "may have proved that certain kinds of movies anyhow are better on the page that they can ever be on the screen."[38]

The Man Within (*The Smugglers* in the United States), was adapted in 1947 and was the first of Greene's novels to be filmed in color. Some years earlier Greene had sold the film rights for a token payment to Ralph Keene. They had made *The New Britain* and *The Future's in the Air* together, and Keene told Greene that with this book he had the chance of making his first feature film. "Well," Greene later commented, "at least he made a profit from the resale to Mr. Box, and Mr. Box made his film with an extraordinary script [by Muriel and Sydney Box] which showed torture with branding irons as part of the nineteenth-century legal system."[39] *The Man Within* was a stylized costume piece, directed by Bernard Knowles, that purported to concern itself with the psychological complexities of its main characters, Andrews (Richard Attenborough), Carlyon (Michael Redgrave), and Elizabeth (Jean Kent). In fact, it was a vast oversimplification of the novel, though the story had a certain excitement. Intended for adults, one suspects it was more popular among younger audiences. Its smugglers' intrigues and misty burials made it often reminiscent of the stories of Greene's distant relative Robert Louis Stevenson.

The last of the films produced between *Went the Day Well?* and *Brighton Rock* was *The Fugitive*. Upon its release in 1947 it was dubbed by one critic "the most pretentious travesty of a literary work since *For Whom the Bell Tolls*."[40] Greene had admired the previous work of John Ford and thought *The Power and the Glory* to be in good hands, but to his dismay Ford turned the novel's protagonist, whom he called the fugitive, into a "pious and heroic priest: the drunkenness had been drained away and the illegitimate child . . . became the bastard of the police-officer who pursued the priest."[41] The banality of Dudley Nichols's screenplay was equaled only by the acting of Henry Fonda as the priest, who "played . . . as though he were half asleep."[42] Most reviewers agreed that the film made a mockery of the original.

By the time Greene undertook to adapt *Brighton Rock* in 1947, he had been associated with the cinema for several years. The earlier films had been disappointing, but with the exception of *Twenty-one Days*, which in any case the censors had prevented from being a serious work, his involvement with them had been minimal. *Brighton Rock* brought a new challenge. It was an ideal novel for the common poetic cinema. As a thriller the story had immediate appeal. It was both exciting and called for mass response. This level supported that other level where the possibility of the poetic lay. The ethical world of right and wrong formed a familiar base from which the theological world of good and evil could be developed.

Brighton Rock remains one of the best adaptations of a Greene novel. The atmosphere of the original is re-created with great precision, and the plot of the story is relatively unchanged. Perhaps a clue to director John Boulting's success is the way he "saw" the novel when he first read it. For him "it was a film. The setting was not a backdrop; it was one of the characters."[43] With this insight into Greene's style Boulting treated the details of the Brighton setting with the same respect he did the characterizations and filmed several sequences directly from the novel.

The film and novel open with the same montage. The camera catches the trains arriving "from Victoria every five minutes." People "rocked down Queen's Road standing on the tops of little local trams, stepped off in bewildered multitudes into fresh and glittering air: the new silver paint sparkled on the piers, . . . a race in miniature motors, a band playing, flower gardens in bloom, . . . an aeroplane advertising something for the health in pale vanishing clouds across the sky."[44] Similarly, the racetrack scene, which was shot at the Brighton Race Course with the technical advice of a former razor carrier for Sabini, the gangster on whom Colleoni was based, follows the novel's description carefully.

Prewar Brighton, with its holiday makers, its piers and racetrack, its obvious juxtaposition of vacation crowds and seamy subworld activities, needed little change. Greene's description had been "a labour of love. . . . No city before the war, not London, Paris or Oxford, had such a hold on my affections," he says.

> I knew it first as a child of six when I was sent with an aunt to convalesce after some illness. . . . Though Nelson Place has been cleared away since the war, and the Brighton race gangs were to all intents quashed forever as a serious menace at Lewes Assizes a little before the date of my novel, and even Sherry's dance hall has vanished, they certainly did exist; there *was* a real slum called Nelson Place, and a man was kidnapped on Brighton front in a broad daylight of the thirties. . . . Colleoni, the gang leader, had his real prototype.[45]

The film, which was shot on location, something not common in the British industry in 1947, captured it all. Greene's Brighton provided for the common cinema at its best: fast, exciting, and engaging.

But what of the poetic, which in the novel lies in the tension between Pinkie's religious beliefs and his social predicament? The film easily picks up his religiosity—in his choice of a doll rather than cigarettes for a prize at the shooting gallery, because she reminds him of the church; in his belief that his marriage to Rose will not be a real marriage, "not like when a priest says it"; in his short discussion with her about "Hell, Flames and damnation." These are the marks of religious belief. Juxtaposed with the agnostic world of Pinkie's gang, they show the terrible tension between his faith and his social aspirations. But the contrast does not explain the deep meaning of that paradox: it only suggests it.

Pinkie's problem originates in Nelson Place. His greatest fear is that he will never escape its failure, depression, poverty, and dullness. Even his sexual problems, associated as they are with his parents' Saturday-night habits, are sociological in nature. As a Catholic, Pinkie connects sex with reproduction—"Saturday nights: and then the birth, the child, habit, and hate."[46] In a very real way sex represents that inevitable return to the hell of poverty he will do anything to escape. Boulting captures this part of Pinkie's predicament admirably. By juxtaposing images of his social situation with those of his faith, Boulting easily makes us sympathetic to Pinkie's bind—for him to save himself from his inheritance of prewar poverty, he must damn himself in the larger Catholic reality.

That is part of the novel's tension. But Greene goes on; while asking us to choose between hells, he makes it clear from the first that Pinkie will fail. Because Nelson Place is a sociopsychological original sin that compels Pinkie to crime, his success in this world depends upon his failure in the next, and vice versa. One way or the other he is damned from the first, like Annie Collins. As Dallow says about her pregnancy: "It does happen. . . . It's the luck of the game."[47]

The problem is, we become sympathetic to Pinkie's social predicament. If Colleoni succeeds at crime, why should not Pinkie reap some of the same comfort and respectability? Here the film fails to catch Greene's footwork. It is not Pinkie's bad luck at being poor that causes his downfull but his massive lack of understanding of the intricacies of social injustice. What torments him to the end is why, when he does what Colleoni does, he is doomed. This is what makes him hold Catholicism so close: somewhere, he believes, there are laws that will show Ida and Colleoni his worth, somewhere there is reason. But in his novel Greene makes it clear that Pinkie is misguided; there is no ultimate justice for him. As Rose walks rapidly toward "the worst horror of all," [48] the priest's suggestion that her love may have saved Pinkie is obliterated. Colleoni lives on at the Metropole: Pinkie is "whipped away into zero—nothing."[49]

The film, however, turns the blow with a scratched record. The anonymity of the confessional is replaced by a clean convent room, the priest, who "had a whistle in his breath,"[50] by a motherly nun. Despite Greene's script directive that the scene "must be done with complete realism from sentimentality,"[51] Rose's face is happy when she listens to the "I love you—I love you—I love you," and the camera moves in for that final shot of the crucifix. Although Boulting felt the shot added an ironic comment on Rose's faith, which he found too naïve, the image gave the film a vaguely happy ending. It added the hope that God's mercy, which we are told is appallingly strange, will somehow prevent Rose from hearing the rest of the recording.

One cannot help questioning this change, which so diminishes the power of the story by destroying the paradox of Pinkie's life. In interviews in both 1948 and 1970, Greene took sole responsibility for ending the film "in a convent nursing-home with a nun speaking the words of hope and comfort which in the book had been uttered by the priest." Only when he saw the rushes did he realize she would have been more effective had she been old and withered, exactly opposite to what she was.[52] But earlier he had indicated the censors were to blame for any diminution of the theme by objecting to "various passages in the dialogue of a specifically religious nature. . . . one is allowed a certain latitude in using the name of God as an expletive, but any serious quotation from the Bible is not permissible."[53]

John Boulting's memory is rather different. According to him, the changes in the last scene were agreed upon by himself and Greene in an attempt to soften the final effect. "We wanted to maintain the horror without the brutality," he says; "the censors were not involved."[54]

Which recollection is the more accurate is relatively unimportant. What is clear is that, for whatever reason, Greene suggested the final changes himself and, though disappointed by them, has been willing over the years to defend the film. The first time this became necessary was when Reg Whitley attacked it in the *Daily Mirror* as "false, cheap, nasty sensationalism. . . . The subtle religious theme," he wrote, "that Graham Greene wove into the life of a boy leader of a Brighton race gang—and gave his novel some justification for being written—has not been put over in the film. Instead, there are ninety-two minutes of murder, brutality, beating-up. And the characters with perhaps one exception, are unpleasant people."[55]

Greene replied to the reproach with a defense that Boulting considers "very honest and very generous—very fair of him."[56] "I can assure your critic," he wrote, "that John Boulting worked quite as hard as myself to retain the religious theme. . . . I should have said that what your critic describes almost too kindly as 'the subtle religious theme' was as present in the film as in the book."[57] More recently he reaffirmed this defense and added that he liked even the film's ending. But he has also indicated some latent dissatisfaction with *Brighton Rock* in saying that "the Boulting brothers were too generous in giving an apprentice his rope."[58]

How exactly the film might have been strengthened without changing its softened conclusion is difficult to say. Greene is right that the novel's religious theme is brought off fairly well, except in the last scenes. When he later wrote the script for *The Third Man* (1949), he and Carol Reed had one of their only arguments over that film's ending. Once again Greene wanted to lighten the blow, which he subsequently did in the endings of several of his later movies, among them *The Comedians* (1967). Since there are almost twenty years between these pictures, one wonders whether, despite his call for poetic cinema, Greene has not felt the persistent though injudicious necessity to reduce the impact of his work when it reached the screen. He has certainly exercised bad judgment about casting. He fought strenuously against having Richard Attenborough play Pinkie, though he how admits Attenborough was perfect for the part. And Elizabeth Taylor was his choice for Martha in *The Comedians*, a choice that was unfortunate, to say the least.

Brighton Rock is a thoroughly credible film. As an adaptation, its fault is its inability to bind the social, philosophic, and psychological levels of the story tightly together, and this is probably caused by a restriction of the medium. The best example of this disability is Pinkie's death. Here the various levels must be so irrevocably joined that the contrast between the boy's "panic and pain" as he goes over the cliff and his final silence, "as if he'd been withdrawn suddenly by a hand out of any existence—past or present . . . ,"[59] must be so poignant that it will trigger at once a sharp acceptance of the necessity of his annihilation, and a recognition of the injustice of his appalling descent into hell. The catalyst Greene uses in the novel is the vitriol. As it blinds Pinkie, it connects him to a long line of tragic heroes.

But if the vitriol, which seems "visual," operates as a pivot in the book, it does not in the film. Greene thought the blinding of his protagonist too horrible for the cinema and kept the bottle in Pinkie's pocket. One might argue that once again his cinematic reasoning was ill-founded, but one cannot argue that the blinding of Pinkie on film would have had the same effect on the viewer as it did on the reader. Because the three levels of the story have not conclusively met in the film, the vitriol simply signals his fear and impotence. In or out of Pinkie's pocket, it cannot be used as it is in the novel to explain the metaphysical force of those feelings.

Although the deep complexity of Pinkie's character remained unrevealed, the film was initially a tremendous success. During its opening week at the Wardour Cinema in London it came within £10 of the record house take. The BBC proposed a radio version, and the film received very favorable reviews. But despite this early interest, *Brighton Rock* ended a financial failure. Boulting attributes its ultimate lack of success to the unreadiness of audiences to accept the film's seedy realism, especially American audiences, who saw the film only three years after the British. In the United States, *Brighton Rock* was retitled *Young Scarface* in reminiscence of Howard Hawks's gangster classic. It received poor reviews and had a very limited showing.

Nevertheless, *Brighton Rock* established two things: Greene's ability to create a valid cinematic experience and the realization that his fiction could survive the change into another medium with at least partial success. After it Greene moved to a greater and more intimate involvement with film. Within the next two years his best movies, *The Fallen Idol* and *The Third Man*, appeared.

3

With Carol Reed:
1948 and 1949

"*Midshipman Easy*," Greene wrote in his *Spectator* column in 1936, "is the first film of a new English director, Mr. Carol Reed, who has more sense of the cinema than most veteran British directors. . . . It is simply and dramatically cut, it contains the best fight I can remember on the screen, and I can imagine no child too sophisticated to be excited and amused."[1] Before the end of Greene's tenure as reviewer he had offered Reed his "unreserved" esteem,[2] compared him with G. W. Pabst,[3] and commended him for taking his camera "beyond the dialogue" in films that were "thoroughly workmanlike and unpretentious, with just a hint of a personal manner."[4] This was steady praise from a trenchant critic.

A decade later Korda introduced the two men and suggested they collaborate on a film. Their association is now cinema history. *The Fallen Idol* won the British Film Industry's Prize for Best Actor, Director, Screenplay, and British Film in 1948; the New York

Critics' Award for Best Director in 1949; the National Board of
Review's Award for Best Actor in 1949; and the Danish Oscar at
Copenhagen in 1950. *The Third Man* took both the Grand Prix and
the Prize For Best Director at Cannes in 1949, The U.S. Directors'
Guild Quarterly Award in 1949, the Academy Award for best
black-and-white cinematography in 1950, and Second Prize at
Copenhagen in 1950.

Their first film, *The Fallen Idol*, was not written for the movies.
Greene recalled that "it was published as *The Basement Room* in 1935
and conceived on a cargo steamer on the way home from Liberia to
relieve the tedium of the voyage." He was surprised when a film of
the story was suggested because it seemed to him that "the subject
matter was unfilmable—a murder committed by the most sympathetic character and an unhappy ending"—and that it would imperil
Korda's investment. But the project went ahead, "and in the conferences that ensued the story was quietly changed, so that the subject
no longer concerned a small boy who unwittingly betrayed his best
friend to the police, but dealt instead with a small boy who believed
that his friend was a murderer and nearly procured his arrest by
telling lies in his defence."[5]

The setting was moved from the large Belgravia house of a wealthy
Englishman to an embassy in the same district. Philip became Felipe
(played by Bobby Henrey), his father, an ambassador. Emmy, the
girl whom Baines (Ralph Richardson) loved, reemerged as Julie
(Michèle Morgan), an embassy typist. MacGregor, Felipe's pet
snake, was introduced. And the ending, whose filmic potential
Greene had questioned, was altered. In the story Philip does not
return quietly to childhood. Greene's final paragraph, and an earlier
premonition of the conclusion—"life fell on him with savagery: you
couldn't blame him if he never faced it again in sixty years"[6]—
indicate an irrevocable and unmerciful fall from innocence to adult-
hood.

Greene has difficulty remembering who made which of the
changes. He attributes the embassy setting to Reed. Both men "felt
that the large Belgravia house was already in these post-war years a
period piece." Greene "fought the solution for awhile and then
wholeheartedly concurred." He worked out the cross-examination of
Julie beside the bed she had shared with Baines and, liking snakes,
introduced MacGregor, which Reed opposed. Both men agreed on

the effectiveness of the clock winder, a witty suggestion that was Reed's.[7]

Such sympathetic dissensions over detail indicate something of the richness of this working partnership. Greene trusted Reed's "sense of the cinema,"[8] and Reed believed that his own ideas were not particularly important. "What counts is the story value," he said, "and the characterization. Certain people want to put over their own ideas about life and politics on film, but I believe that a director has no right to inflict his amateur politics and opinions on an audience. . . . My job is to convey to the audience what the author had in mind."[9] But, he added on another occasion, "you've got to be willing to sit with him, to say, . . . 'We could do this with a look rather than dialogue . . . .' Letting an inexperienced screenwriter—even when he's an experienced novelist or playwright—work alone won't do. . . . I can be of help in interpreting the writer's ideas."[10] So he and Greene "worked closely together, covering so many feet of carpet a day, acting scenes at each other. No third ever joined our conferences," Greene reported. "So much value lies in the clear cut-and-thrust of argument between two people."[11]

Reed's ability to combine his director's talents with Greene's ideas is most obvious in his portrayal of Felipe. The casting of the boy was of upmost importance because the whole film rests on his credibility, and for this Reed was entirely responsible. As Greene wrote, Reed had an "extraordinary feeling for the right face for the right part."[12] But it was not only in choosing Bobby Henrey, who was nine and had never seen a movie camera, that Reed exercised his skills. With him he performed what film critic Dilys Powell called "a miracle of creative direction."[13] His method was to tell the child nothing of the plot during the film's shooting. Instead he invented a game whereby Henrey remembered some words and then ran or walked, looking happy or sad when he spoke them. After the scene was filmed, Reed told him another set of words, and another sequence was shot. The result is "not simply that the boy never makes a wrong gesture or uses a wrong intonation; he is never *seen* wrong; the delicate complex of his relations with a confusing world is flawlessly apprehended."[14]

From *The Fallen Idol*'s first shot of Felipe looking down through the stair railing to the vividly checkered hallway floor below, we find ourselves in the world of childhood as *Greene* sees it. Reed reinforces this world of isolation, "of moral chaos . . . in which the ignorance and weakness of the many allows complete mastery of the few,"[15] by playing, as Greene so often does in his writing, on the relationship between character and setting. In using the stair railing, for example, to separate visually the worlds of innocence and experience, he strengthens our sense of the child's imprisonment among adults.

We frequently adopt Felipe's point of view and look with him through the railing to the lower hall. It is from behind these "bars" we often hear the Baineses argue, from this position we see the fight that precipitates Mrs. Baines's fall, and from here we watch the child's mother return. On other occasions we assume a vantage point in the adult world watching from below as the boy performs on the upper side of the railing. From the lower hall we catch his troubled face after Mrs. Baines has forced him to disclose his secret with Baines, and from here we see him run onto the landing and shout to his friend. By changing our point of view in this way, Reed gives us a remarkable picture of the confusion and loneliness of childhood.

Felipe's isolation is intensified by Reed's use of the S or snake shape of the staircase as a central emblem in the film's patterned imagery. The stairs occasion the boy's loss of innocence: before Mrs. Baines falls over the railing, he watches from behind the "bars," isolated and protected from the adult world below. After the fall he enters that world and stands at the bottom of the stairs to tell his lies to the police. He returns to his former position behind the railing only after the adults have rejected his story, and with it the truth, and remains there confused and alienated to await his mother's return.

Dramatically, Felipe's loss of innocence is the result of a series of disillusionments that begins when Baines asks him to keep secret the meeting with Julie. Reed enhances the narrative by setting it against the symbolically suggestive snake shape of the stairs so that we connect their shape with MacGregor the snake and the snake with Felipe's loss of innocence when Mrs. Baines falls. By adapting the literary allusion occasioned by MacGregor to his cinematic purposes, Reed fuses the dramatic with the visual, making the stairs far more important in the film than they are in the story. We see them not only as a means of getting from one floor to another but as an integral visual part of the action.

Reed does not use the snake symbolically as a writer would, but we make something like symbolic connections when we see him. We notice that MacGregor is present in all the scenes in which Julie and

Baines are together before Mrs. Baines's plot to catch them begins to work: he is in the boy's pocket in the tea room; he is talked about both at the zoo and at supper; he is killed by Mrs. Baines with a vengeance equal to that she feels toward her husband and Julie. As Felipe's imprisonment and disillusionment are fixed visually with the stairs, so the snake is the visual focus for the lovers' relationship; it is where they are, and they are part of the working out of Felipe's fall from innocence.

One does not like to overemphasize the imagistic connections of the piece, for the camera work is always dramatically well founded—Reed insisted that "technique for its own sake . . . serves no purpose in film"[16]—but at the same time one is forced to make certain visual links that go beyond the main narrative. The dart, for example, that Felipe makes with Mrs. Baines's telegram is shot at the lovers. This produces a visible counterpart of what the telegram is intended to do—catch Baines and Julie together and terminate their relationship. Similarly, when the dart lands in the rosebush, a concealed place where the doctor can later unexpectedly find it, it simultaneously forms an image of the lovers' sexual union.

These effects are largely Reed's work. What is remarkable about them is the way they constantly reinforce Greene's conception of a child's world cut off from the mainstream of events by lack of communication and ignorance. They show how a director who believed that his films should "be true . . . to the characters they are portraying, and let the technique suit itself to the material at hand"[17] can accentuate an author's idea by drawing out what is easily filmable and using it to reinforce what may appear "visual" on the page but is not necessarily cinematic.

Reed was particularly adept at this. In Greene's story the sequence where Mrs. Baines wakes Philip and demands to know where Julie is, reads:

> . . . he opened his eyes and Mrs. Baines was there, her grey untidy hair in threads over his face, her black hat askew. A loose hairpin fell on the pillow and one musty thread brushed his mouth. "Where are they?" she whispered. "Where are they?"
> Philip watched her in terror. [18]

The emphasis, despite the visual quality of the passage, is on the question "Where are they?" When filmed, however, the hairpin dropping on the pillow tells everything. It signals Mrs. Baines's extreme irritation, for her usually immaculate hair must be askew if a pin falls, and indicates Felipe's terror. The consequence is that her words become almost irrelevant; we know what she will say before we even see her. Reed rightly uses the falling hairpin to its full cinematic advantage. With it he sets the tone and tells the story. Here his camera acts, as Greene noted it did in *Laburnum Grove*, "with a kind of quick shrewd independence of the dialogue and presents its own equally dramatic commentary."[19]

Another example of a different though equally effective method Reed uses to reinforce Greene's ideas is in the filming of Felipe's entry into the tea room. Greene writes:

> It occurred to Philip that it would be amusing to imitate Mrs. Baines's voice and call "Baines" to him from the door.
>
> It shrivelled them; you couldn't describe it in any other way; it made them smaller, they weren't happy any more and they weren't bold. Baines was the first to recover and trace the voice, but that didn't make things as they were. The sawdust was spilled out of the afternoon; nothing you did could mend it, and Philip was scared.[20]

Reed allows the dialogue to carry its full weight. His camera, again moving independently, composes a backdrop for the child's call. With it he records everything in the tea shop, even "the wasps driving like small torpedoes across the pane."[21] The visual circumstances in which Felipe's shout is made support his outburst and make us acutely aware of the nature of the relationship between Baines and Julie. Reed's knowledge that "very often a brilliant line is worth more than any number of images, no matter how eloquently composed,"[22] makes the scene effective. He trusts Greene's dialogue to stand on its own and frees his camera to record a separate, but dramatically parallel, commentary.

Yet as astute as Reed is at interpreting Greene's text, changes of intent still occur. Here is the same scene before Philip enters to shout "Baines":

> It was the pink sugar cakes in the window on a paper doily, the ham, the slab of mauve sausage, the wasps driving like small torpedoes across the pane that caught Philip's attention. His feet were tired by pavements; he had been afraid to cross the road, had simply walked first in one direction, then in the other. He was nearly home now; the square was at the end of the street; this was a shabby outpost of Pimlico, and he smudged the pane with his nose looking for sweets, and saw between the

cakes and ham a different Baines. He hardly recognised the bulbous eyes, the bald forehead.[23]

As we read, Baines's situation becomes evident. First we have the setting: " . . . the pink sugar cakes in the window on a paper doily, the ham, the slab of mauve sausage." Then we see Baines "between the cakes and ham." But his "bulbous eyes" and "bald forehead" have combined with "the pink sugar cakes" and "the slab of mauve sausage," and he is "hardly recognised." The concrete details of the set have merged into an *abstract* image of a man in a predicament that forebodes no pleasant ending.

In its use of concrete detail the image seems particularly visual. When it is cinematically reproduced, however, its meaning is altered. When we see the window and Felipe in Reed's film, we understand Baines's situation immediately, but we draw our conclusions from the expression on his face and from the secluded place he has chosen for his tête-à-tête with Julie. Reed's and Greene's descriptions begin with the same objects. Reed's camera records their surface value. He observes them as the eye would, controlling the observation by the camera's position, the focus of the lens, and so on. He is thus able to make us see first the pink cakes and ham as Greene does and then, by changing the depth of focus, Baines's head behind the window. This is a literal and careful visual reproduction of the original description.

The prose, however, departs from what the eye sees and invests the objects with other properties. Our imaginations cannot accept the surface value of the situation as our eye must, and the doily, ham, sugar cakes, bulbous eyes, and bald forehead coalesce into an imaginative pattern. Greene's literary trope is achieved; we are left with a multidimensional image of Baines caught in a grotesque and inextricable trap.

Perhaps the result is similar as far as plot development goes. In both treatments we have seen a new Baines and have understood that if Mrs. Baines were to discover what is going on he would be in trouble. But on film, because we simply accept the cakes, ham, and sausage as what they are, we do not make the connections between them and Baines that Greene intends in his prose. The parts of the scene do not merge into an image, and the result is that our understanding of Baines is impoverished.

If we continue with the scene to where Philip shouts out in

imitation of Mrs. Baines, we are provided with another example. When we read of the encounter, from the boy's call, our imaginations "trace" the scene to create a "shrivelled," "spilled out" atmosphere. Only Philip's fear marks how totally the "happy, bold and buccaneering Baines" has been deflated. There are no facial expressions, no background details to hamper us in experiencing the scene. Philip's call sets our imaginations loose, and, like Baines, we "trace" the perimeter of the arena.

As in the earlier part of the sequence, Greene's image is expansive. The words explode, and we make imaginary combinations of them. "Shrivelled" and "smaller" fuse with Philip's inability to "mend" things, and Baines comes to resemble the afternoon with its "sawdust . . . spilled out." The cinematic image works in a different way: it concretizes; it does not abstract. By juxtaposing the physical details of the tea shop, Reed makes us aware of the illicit nature of Baines's and Julie's relationship. He shows us Felipe's awkwardness in the situation, but he does not make us feel the sense of deflation Greene describes. The visual minutiae Reed records condition and limit our reaction. Greene's prose does the reverse. It offers us a broader, multifaceted image of Baines's situation.

This is not to say that film is inferior to prose but to show that it works in a different way. Even before Eisenstein's slaughter sequence in *Strike*, cinema history is filled with examples of how concrete visual images may be used to spark viewers' imaginations into seeing what their eyes do not. *The Fallen Idol* is no exception. When Reed uses the snake, interestingly a literary allusion, and the snake-shaped staircase to add depth to the narrative, he does precisely this. Yet in the tea-shop scene, where he adapts literally, the full impact of Greene's words eludes the screen.

Nevertheless, Reed is so masterful at restoring organic unity to the story that Greene claims *The Fallen Idol* to be his favourite screen work, because it is "more a writer's film than a director's."[24] The power of the movie lies not in the exact reproduction of individual sequences, though they are there, but in the overall transposition of Greene's sympathetic characterizations and superb control. Reed manages a flawless picture of Greene's protagonist, lonely as he sneaks ginger beer and listens to his idol's stories, innocent as he enters into terrifying secrets, frightened as he watches what he believes to be a murder, loyal as he lies to protect Baines, and confused as he threatens his friend with the truth.

Reed uses Felipe's credulity as a foil for Mrs. Baines's asperity. Playing one against the other, he quickly establishes Mrs. Baines as the warden of Felipe's childhood. From the first we know that

> you couldn't laugh at Mrs. Baines. She wasn't Sir Hubert Reed, who used steel nibs and carried a penwiper in his pocket; she wasn't Mrs. Wince-Dudley; she was darkness when the night-light went out in a draught; she was the frozen blocks of earth he had seen one winter in a graveyard when someone said, "They need an electric drill"; she was the flowers gone bad and smelling in the little closet room at Penstanley. There was nothing to laugh about. You had to endure her. . . .[25]

Her presence pervades the film and makes both the other characters and the audience apprehensive.

But she is not the most evil person in Felipe's world. That position is reserved for Baines, who, like many of Greene's other characters, harbors a paradoxical mixture of good and evil. In his warm and sympathetic way it is he who introduces Felipe to deceit with his lies about Africa and Julie. Here Reed's ability to match Greene's narrative control is of upmost importance, for Baines must be seen alternately as openhearted and panic-stricken as he plays hero to Felipe and prey to Mrs. Baines.

Reed's success in transposing these custodians of the child's happiness lies largely in his making use of environments that reflect the characters' personalities. Outside the embassy Mrs. Baines would appear little more than a compulsively neat, unpleasant woman, but stealing her way through its large, darkened central hall with its sharply defined checkered floor and sheet-draped furniture, she becomes a ghostly presence, an absorbing fear.

On film the distinction between man and object is obliterated; they are interchangeable. Greene uses this cinematic principle in his writing, joining the animate and inanimate to create atmosphere and character. In transposing Greene, Reed is working with what is essentially a cinematic process put to literary use. His great ability is in controlling the tension between the animate and inanimate so skillfully that he catches the propulsive relationship between character and setting in Greene's work.

Reed's skill in this respect is even more imperative in *The Third Man*, where Harry Lime looms into existence only near the end of the movie and then wrapped in the atmospheric density of various impressions. This larger-than-life character is created almost entirely from reminiscences and empirical minutiae: the elaborate furnishings of his flat, the two statues guarding his door, the dice Anna fingers beside his telephone, the cat playing with his shoelace, the collection of papers and photos Calloway shows concerning his crimes. Greene allows us to move back and forth among separate impressions of Lime as one would between paintings in an exhibition. Each has its own composition and detail but is connected to the others by theme. As Calloway says of Martins, and might well of us: "It was odd how like the Lime he knew was to the Lime I knew: it was only that he looked at Lime's image from a different angle or in a different light."[26]

Unlike *The Fallen Idol*, *The Third Man* was intended for the cinema from the first. "Like many love affairs it started at a dinner table and continued with many headaches in many places: Vienna, Venice, Ravello, London, Santa Monica."[27] In late 1947 Korda asked Greene to write a second film for Reed, to be set in occupied Vienna divided into Russian, American, French, and British zones with an internationally policed center, the Inner Stadt, the city itself deep within Communist territory, joined to the West by a narrow corridor. Korda wanted to put this complex situation on film.

At the time all Greene had to offer was an opening paragraph scratched down years before on the flap of an envelope: "I had paid my last farewell to Harry a week ago, when his coffin was lowered into the frozen February ground, so that it was with incredulity that I saw him pass by, without a sign of recognition, among the host of strangers in the Strand."[28] This idea was to provide the key incident for the film.

Greene went to Vienna in search of the rest of the story in February, 1948, and was frustrated on the first visit as he waited for inspiration that would not come, soaking up detail but unable to discover either plot or character. He had allowed himself two weeks in Vienna. With three days left he had no story, "not even the story-teller."[29] Then suddenly, on the day before his departure, things began to fall into place. A young British intelligence officer told him about the Vienna sewer system that undercut the military zones, and they visited the sewers; over lunch he also mentioned the penicillin racket. That night Greene had dinner with a friend, the novelist Elizabeth Bowen, who had come to Vienna to lecture for the British Council; he took her to the Oriental, probably the most seedy nightclub she had ever been in, and predicted the place would be raided, which it was, providing her with the most dramatic midnight entertainment she had in Vienna.[30]

These important elements, together with the opening paragraph and the bits of photogenic background he had been absorbing, combined to give Greene his story. He left the next day for Venice to write it up. When he returned to Vienna with Reed three months later to turn his idea into film, he found, to his embarrassment, that the city had "completely changed. The blackmarket restaurants . . . were now serving legal if frugal meals. The ruins had been cleared away from in front of the Café Mozart." Over and over again he found himself saying to Carol Reed, " 'But I assure you Vienna was really like that—three months ago.' "[31]

As Vienna had changed, so would Greene's story. Although conceived for the cinema, it was given birth as a prose treatment that "was never written to be read." Greene felt it "impossible to capture for the first time in the dull shorthand of a script" that "measure of characterisation, . . . mood and atmosphere" which the film would require.[32] *The Third Man*, therefore, began as a story and went through what Greene felt to be "interminable transformations from one treatment to another"[33] before it reached the screen.

These transformations can best be traced in the Humanities Research Center, in Austin, Texas, where five manuscripts of the film play are housed. They are: the "Story" (dated June 2, 1948, and 127 pages long), the "Treatment," which is the first script (undated and 120 pages), the "First Draft Script" (undated and 128 pages), the "Second Draft Script" (dated September 20, 1948, and 98 pages), and the "Release Script" (undated and 173 pages).

Typical of the transformations that so irritated Greene and made him long for his old job as novelist—"that one-man business where I bear full responsibility for failure"[34]—are the many changes in names, nationalities, and status of his characters. Scarcely one of them remained the same. Cast as Rollo Martins, hero of the story, Hollywood actor Joseph Cotten objected to the name, which to an "American ear apparently involved homosexuality." The name was changed to Holly, in memory of "that figure of fun, the nineteenth-century American poet Thomas Holley Chivers."[35] Martins's nationality, British at the start, then Canadian in the draft scripts, became American. Cooler, Harry Lime's colleague in crime in the "Story" became Tyler in the "Draft Scripts" and finally Popescu in the film when his citizenship was changed from American to Rumanian "in deference to American opinion, . . . since Orson Welles's engagement had already supplied us with one American villain";[36] in the "Story," Lime, like Martins, had been British. Lime's girl friend, Anna Schmidt, initially Hungarian with false Austrian papers, became first Estonian, then Czechoslovakian; the false papers remained. Mr. Kurtz became Baron Kurtz. British Intelligence officer Colonel Calloway was demoted to major, though his Russian counterpart, invented specially for the film, held the rank of colonel. British Council representative Crabbin—incorrectly called Crabbit throughout the published version of the film script (printed by Lorrimer in 1969)—was given military rank and, somewhere between the "First Draft Script" and the "Second Draft Script" was split into two, becoming Captain Tombs and Captain Carter. These parts were to be played by Basil Radford and Naunton Wayne but were eventually reunited for the film as just Crabbin, played by Wilfred Hyde-White.

Besides these changes the plot too underwent many alterations. Some were minor additions: the cat that nestles at Lime's feet in the doorway, Kurtz's dog, the cuckoo-clock speech (Orson Welles's invention). Others were deletions: the mix-up between Buck Dexter, Martins's pseudonym as a writer of Westerns, and Benjamin Dexter, the British writer; and the Russian attempt to kidnap Anna. The order of some sequences was changed, the dialogue was tightened, and the beginning and ending were reworked several times.

Greene's "Story" opens with a narrator telling us: "One never knows when the blow may fall. When I saw Rollo Martins first I made this note on him for my security police files." Adding, "If you are to understand this strange, rather sad story you must have an impression at least of the background," the narrator goes on to describe everything he points out in the film.

This beginning is similar to that of the movie, but before reaching its final form, it was changed many times. The first script, the "Treatment," begins in Calloway's office. "You want to hear about the case of Harry Lime?" Calloway asks. "It's an ugly story if you leave out the girl." A montage of postwar Vienna follows, of ruined buildings, notices in four languages, marching soldiers, food parcels being thrown to singers at the opera, the Great Wheel of the Prater revolving slowly above the park. Calloway describes "the sad smashed city of Vienna" and points to a wall map. The scene dissolves to Martins looking over the city from his airplane window and again to the plane landing. Martins hands his passport to an immigration officer; a stewardess offers his name. A reporter for the *Morning News* wants to write a profile of him and ends up giving him money for a taxi. The script cuts to Harry Lime's flat.

The opening of the "First Draft Script" is the same except there is no stewardess, and Martins runs from Beale, the reporter, to catch a bus, shouting, "They wouldn't know me!" The "Second Draft Script" opens with Martins boarding a plane for Vienna. He is warned by a vice-consul: "Remember, Vienna is an occupied city." Shot two, from outside the airport, shows "the Constellation warming up." The credits are superimposed on a series of shots "establishing the progress of Martins's journey": Martins in his seat, an aerial shot of the ocean, Martins eating, night over the ocean, Martins dozing, the plane over Paris, French customs officers, Martins boarding another plane, an aerial shot of the beginning of the Alps, Martins sleeping and unshaven, Martins feeling ill, more customs officials, Martins looking out of the plane window, Vienna. A map of the four occupied zones is superimposed on the aerial view of the city. Passengers disembark, and Martins is questioned by a British officer about the reason for his trip.

With the exception of a name change for Rollo, this opening is the same as that in the "Shooting Script," Reed's copy of which is housed in the British Film Institute Library, in London. Three months after the film was completed, he, Korda and David O. Selznick, the film's American coproducer, decided that the first sequences were confusing and reshot them in Korda's studio at Shepperton.

The finished film begins with the credits rolling over a huge close-up of the strings of a zither to the accompaniment of the "Harry Lime Theme." A high-angle shot of Vienna is superimposed by the title "Vienna," which fades out as the commentary, read by Reed in the British version, Cotten in the American, commences: "I never knew the old Vienna before the War with its Strauss music, its glamour and easy charm. . . . I really got to know it in the classic period of the Black Market." Boots, socks, watches, and packages of tea change hands. A body floats in the river. English, Russian, and French posters form the backdrop as the narrator describes Vienna's four zones. A jeepload of guards passes. Soldiers march through bombed areas, and a train pulls into the station. Martins descends looking for Lime.

This opening is closer to the original "Story" than are any of the subsequent versions and is reminiscent of the montage John Boulting used in 1947 to open *Brighton Rock*. It clarifies what had become a confused beginning to the film by rapidly acquainting viewers with the story's background. It also shortens the movie by removing shots, like those of the Canadian airport and the Eiffel Tower, which were unessential in establishing the story and would have proved visually dull in one of the first films shot in war-ravaged Vienna.

It was over the ending of the film that Greene and Reed had one of their "few major disputes."[37] Greene's "Story" finishes happily with Anna and Martins walking arm in arm from Lime's funeral. In the "Treatment" this ending is modified so that Martins gets out of Calloway's car and "begins to walk back down the road. Calloway turns and watches. In the long street lined with monumental masons [sic] the two little figures slowly come towards each other: the picture fades out." In the "Second Draft Script" the ending was changed again. Here Martins "begins to walk down the road. Calloway turns and watches. Anna is approaching. Martins stops and waits for her. She reaches him and seeks in vain for a word. He makes a gesture with his hand, and she pays no attention, walking right past him and on into the distance. Martins follows her with his eyes. From outside our vision we can hear a car horn blow again and again."

In the film the sequence loosely follows this version: Martins leans against a woodcart and waits for Anna. Leaves fall on the road as she approaches. She passes Martins without a glance. He lights a cigarette. There is a long pause as she walks away, and the movie ends.

This scene's evolution speaks for the difference of opinion about how it should be handled. Greene "held the view that an entertainment of this kind was too light an affair to carry the weight of an unhappy ending. Reed," Greene said, "felt that my ending— indeterminate though it was, with no words spoken—would strike the audience, who had just seen Harry die, as unpleasantly cynical. I admit I was only half convinced; I was afraid few people would wait in their seats during the girl's long walk from the graveside and that they would leave the cinema under the impression that the ending was as conventional as mine and more drawn out." But, Greene concedes, "I had not given enough consideration to the mastery of Reed's direction, and at that stage, of course, we neither of us could have anticipated Reed's brilliant discovery of Mr. Karas, the zither player." Reed, he allows, "has been proved triumphantly right."[38]

These alterations made to the beginning and ending are character-
istic of the kinds of changes that occur when the manifold and
unforeseeable circumstances of production impinge on and transform
the script. Some simply shorten and tighten the narrative. In the
"Story," for example, before Lime's first funeral, Martins is taken on
a long, panoramic taxi ride through the cemetery in order to establish
Harry's Catholicism. In the film the drive becomes unnecessary; a
priest, mumbling Latin beside a grave, comes into focus from the
background, and Lime's religion is instantly settled.

Other alterations change the direction of the narrative slightly and
have to do with the different way words and visual images are
apprehended. Thoughts and feelings in the original, for example,
had to be given physical form. The tension Calloway and Paine feel as
they wait for Lime outside the Café Marcus Auriel is focused on the
balloon man's shadow. Anna's feelings for Harry are witnessed in the
way she plays with his dice. Martins's love for her takes on the shape
of a bunch of flowers.

Some such transformations are less effective than others. In the
scene in Anna's flat the flowers indicate Martins's love, but they do
not tell us what that love means to him. When he tells Calloway in
the "Story," " . . . it wasn't a beautiful face. . . . It was a face to live
with, day in, day out. A face for wear," we understand a great deal.
The statement holds a past, a present, and a future. When he
continues, telling Calloway, "I felt as though I'd come into a new
country where I couldn't speak the language. I always thought it was
beauty one loved in a woman. I stood there at the curtains, waiting to
pull them, looking out. I couldn't see anything but my own face,
looking back into the room, looking for her,"[39] we are involved in
the real nature of love: uniqueness, mystery, the loss of oneself. The
depth of Martins's feelings in this sequence eludes the screen; in fact,
it is never transferred to film.

Reed has similar trouble translating Martins's disorientation when
he finally understands the implications of Harry's crimes. Greene
writes:

> If one watched a world come to an end, a plane dive from its course, I
> don't suppose one would chatter, and a world for Martins had certainly
> come to an end, a world of easy friendship, hero-worship, confidence that
> had begun twenty years before—in a school corridor. Every memory—

afternoons in the long grass, the illegitimate shoots on Brickworth Common, the dreams, the walks, every shared experience was simultaneously tainted, like the soil of an atomised town. One could not walk there with safety for a long while.[40]

To try to translate this would be futile, for every word explodes into a complex image in the reader's mind. The film must have Martins simply drink his whisky (which he also does in the "Treatment," though there the act is reinforced when Calloway tells us, "He obeyed me as though I were his doctor") and leave, relying on earlier explanations about Martins's relations with Harry to carry the viewer through this salient scene.

Reed uses a rapid montage of a microscope, finger prints, threads from a coat, files about Lime, and still photographs, to relate the facts with such shocking swiftness that the viewer cannot help but share a little of Martins's confusion. The extent of his disorientation is not evident, however, until his drunken arrival at Anna's flat several scenes later. Reed does not reduce him, as Greene does in the "Story," to a state of total inactivity in a split second. Greene can juxtapose the abstract concepts of "frienship, hero-worship, confidence" with Calloway's presentation of the evidence and in a few lines produce conditions that stun Martins. But the images in Reed's montage are fixed and cannot work fast enough to capture feelings "that had begun twenty years before." They do not show Martins utterly incapacitated because they cannot supply the intensity of shock that Greene's words do. And so the film must settle for less—Martins's disorientation, evidenced by his drunkenness.

The result is a motivational change. Because Martins is so be-numbed in Greene's "Story," his decision to help Calloway capture Lime is firm. By the end of the famous sequence in the Prater, Martins has decided: "It was like the whole past moving off under a cloud. Martins suddenly called after him, 'Don't trust me, Harry.' "[41] The story's conclusion is well defined and brief: he must tell Anna what has happened, plan and carry through Lime's capture, shoot him in the sewers, bury him.

On film, however, Martins leaves Calloway's office bewildered but not dazed. His decision to help capture Lime is not made from the shock of recognition and release from past romanticisms, causes that make his decision irrevocable. Instead, the cinematic Martins joins Calloway because he wants to help Anna gain her freedom. When she refuses to leave Vienna, the end of the story becomes uncertain. Martins returns to Calloway's office and demands a ticket on "the first plane out of here." The children's-ward sequence is required to reinforce Calloway's already impressive evidence against Lime before Martins can be coerced into waiting for Harry in the Café Marcus Auriel.

The story's altered ending also does more than just make the audience linger and let the final impact of the film sink in. It has a subtle side effect on characterization as well. The Anna who walks away leaving Holly behind her is a more valid character than the one in the "Story" who capriciously slips her hand through his arm. She remains faithful to Harry Lime and his figure, in consequence, becomes larger and more difficult for the audience to contend with. Even such a seemingly innocuous change as the addition of Anna's cat, introduced by Reed to increase suspense in the sequence where Lime is first seen, has its secondary effect. The cat has no interest in Martins; like Anna, it cares only for Lime. When we see it sitting at Harry's feet, its loyalty too increases Harry's human quality for us.

If we look closely, we see that many of the changes apparently made for cinematic reasons also stress the story's theme of divided loyalties, soften Harry's crimes, and make him more human. Another good example is Holly's meeting with Anna after Calloway has shown him Harry's file. In the "Story" he tells Anna about "the children dead with meningitis, and the children in the mental ward" and shows her pictures of Harry's victims. In the "Draft Scripts" Holly says, in the same vein: "They've been stealing penicillin, mixing it with water, I don't know what. People have been dying from it—wounded people, children. . . . Harry made seventy pounds a tube—he ran the business." In the film these specific references are cut. Anna knows of Harry's crimes and has accepted them before Martins arrives. This not only shortens the film but also plays down the lasting shock of Calloway's revelations. In the film the discovery of Harry's villainy is glossed over this way:

> Anna: He told you, didn't he?
> Martins: Told me?
> Anna: About Harry.
> Martins: You know?
> Anna: I've seen Major Calloway today.

This is more than just the "dull shorthand" of a script. It is an alteration that once again changes character, though in this instance it is not occasioned by the aesthetic differences between the word and the visual image. Here Greene's story was redirected for political reasons, to prepare Lime for American audiences. Had he remained British, as in the original, the problem would not have arisen, but when Orson Welles, whom Reed wanted for the part, was cast as Lime, the citizenship had to be changed and things made what David O. Selznick termed "acceptable" for Americans.

In Greene's and Reed's first meeting with Selznick, he complained about the script's title: "Listen, boys," he said, "who the hell is going to a film called *The Third Man*? . . . You can do better than that, Graham. . . . I'm no writer and you are, what we want is something like *Night in Vienna*, a title which will bring them in."[42] He went on to deride the story itself, calling it "sheer buggery, . . . what you learn in your English schools. . . . This guy comes to Vienna looking for his friend. He finds his friend's dead. Right? Why doesn't he go home then?" When Greene argued, "He has a motive of revenge. He has been beaten up by a military policeman," and finally, in desperation, "Within twenty-four hours he's in love with Harry Lime's girl," Selznick repeated his question: "Why didn't he go home before that?"[43]

As the film developed, Selznick became very self-righteous about what he considered to be "acceptable" to an American public. On October 16, 1948, after he had read the "Second Draft Script," he sent a telegram to Betty Goldsmith, his foreign coordinator, in which he stated that the script, though "Basically a very good script" and "as Korda said, a great improvement over the prior draft," was "not satisfactory from the standpoint of the price of the picture or its acceptability to American audiences." In the telegram he demanded that Reed must be made "personally familiar, and in detail, with our rights under the contract" and said it was "absolutely essential that there be an American writer on the job at once . . . who can make the dialogue acceptable from an American standpoint, even if it is not as good as it should be." His telegram continued:

> I certainly am going to insist upon certain basic things on which I spent many, many long hours of wrangling in order to get Reed's and Greene's agreement; thus, for instance, the script is written as though England were the sole occupying power of Vienna, with some Russians vaguely in the distance; with an occasional Frenchman wandering around; and with,

most important from the standpoint of this criticism, the only American being an occasional soldier who apparently is merely part of the British occupying force, plus the heavy (Lime), plus the hero (who is Canadian in some scenes and American in others), plus another American heavy named Tyler. And, just to make matters worse, the American hero apparently is completely subject to the orders and instructions of the British authorities, and behaves as though there were no American whatsoever among the occupying powers, nor any American authority, and indeed as far as this picture is concerned, there is none. It would be little short of disgraceful on our part as Americans if we tolerated this nonsensical handling of the Four-Power occupation of Vienna. . . . I went through this at the greatest length and in the greatest detail with Reed and with Greene, and come hell or high water, I simply will not stand for it in its present form. . . .

I'm sure that Korda told them I knew my business, and that they could count on getting intelligent and helpful suggestions from me; but to follow only what they saw fit to follow. . . . I spent countless hours going through with Reed and Greene, and getting agreement on, the treatment of the whole background of Vienna today, to give the picture size, and more importantly, to give it understandability from the standpoint of American audiences. We laid out in the greatest detail scenes of the changing of authority from one occupying power to another, with the Four Powers in turn changing in the chair; and in order that this might not be extraneous material, we went to the greatest pains to make this material background of the personal story. . . . We frankly made the Russians the heavies, in pursuit of the girl. All of this has been eliminated, even what was in the original script. We must insist upon its return, for patriotic reasons, for purposes of the picture's importance and size . . . and for purposes of our understanding of what on earth is going on in Vienna that these things can be happening?[44]

When Selznick issued a bull, it was usually observed in unqualified obedience. But Greene and Reed appear to have managed their own show with a fine Gallican contempt for edicts from Hollywood. No writer was hired to Americanize the dialogue. True, Tyler's citizenship was changed to Rumanian, but the American presence in Vienna was not made obvious as Selznick had requested, and the Four Power occupation of the city was not clarified until much later, when the film's opening was reshot as much for aesthetic reasons as for any others. In fact, if the alterations made after Selznick's telegram are checked, one sees that practially nothing of what he so vehemently required was done. On the contrary, instead of

the Russians becoming "heavies," or even remaining as heavy as they
had been in the original "Story," they were lightened in the film.

This can best be seen in the episode in which the Russians try to
kidnap Anna, which was eliminated "at a fairly late stage" because,
Greene says, "it was not satisfactorily tied into the story, and it
threatened to turn the film into a propagandist picture."[45] In its
place he and Reed added the later half of scenes 83 (in the Lorrimer
text), where Brodsky asks for Anna's passport, and 106, in which
Calloway warns her of her situation. In these additions we are told
that Anna's papers are forged. This is necessary so that when Martins
later agrees to help Calloway in exchange for her freedom we know
she risks deportation. Lime's deal with the Russians underlines this,
but his deal is in the original, though it is more forcefully presented
there than it is in the film.

Some of the kidnapping sequence does find its way onto the screen,
though Greene's banter in the original about the four nationalities is
almost entirely lost. The scene where Anna is picked up by the
soldiers persists through the "Second Draft Script" in the following
form:

> British M.P.: I'm not staying here. Let the girl dress by herself.
> *He prepares to leave.*
> American M.P.: You can't leave a little goil alone with Rusky here. I'd
> better stay.
> British M.P. *to* French M.P.: You coming, Froggy?
> *The French M.P. is amused and speaks in French.*
> French M.P.: Qu'est-ce-ça fait? [sic] (What does it matter?) I will look
> after both of them.
> *The British M.P. goes out of the room. The American M.P. stays in the room
> and keeps his back chivalrously turned, but he is restless and takes a bit of
> chewing-gum. The French M.P. thinks it fun, lights a cigarette and watches
> with detached, amused interest the attitude of the other two. The Russian M.P. is
> just doing his duty and watches the girl closely all the time without sexual
> interest.*[46]

All that survives of this raillery is the British M.P.'s stubborn
devotion to duty: Anna dresses alone in a dark alcove.

When she arrives at International Headquarters, Calloway in-
tercepts the soldiers before they get to Brodsky and takes her to his
own office. Here he tells her Harry is alive and, in warning her of
Brodsky's designs, tries to discover Lime's whereabouts. The film

moves from here directly to the sequence in front of Kurtz's house, eliminating three of the original scenes. Only the first of these is relevant. It takes place in the hall outside Calloway's office:

> Calloway: The Russians claim the body, Martins.
> Martins: You aren't going to hand her over?
> Calloway: Her papers are false.
> Martins: Why, you double-timing . . .
> Calloway: She's no concern of mine, Martins. It's Lime I want.
> Martins: Damn Lime.[47]

In neither the final script nor the film is Anna turned over to Brodsky.

The result of these changes is obvious. Contrary to Selznick's wishes, the Russian image was softened, though not greatly, and at the same time the clarity of the Viennese situation, in which kidnappings, by Greene's own admission, were "perfectly possible,"[48] was reduced. Greene says simply, "We had no desire to move people's political emotions; we wanted to entertain them, to frighten them a little, to make them laugh."[49]

On the surface this may seem a plausible explanation. But is Greene not a little disingenuous when he would have us believe that it was possible to set a film in postwar Vienna, a British and American coproduction at that, and keep politics out? One might speculate that he and Reed softened the Russian image in the film as a direct counterreaction to Selznick's stormy cold-war attitude, or that, since they had taken steps to humanize the American villain, they decided to restore the balance by devillainizing the Russians, too. Greene's anti-Americanism was, after all, no secret by 1949.

At any rate, although Selznick had a point about the low American profile in Greene's Vienna, Greene and Reed had their way. Selznick's telegram certainly indicates that he expected to have greater influence than he did, and if his expectations were justified, Greene and Reed may have been lucky to get away with making so few political concessions.

According to Greene, a legal loophole helped them manage this. The contract stipulated that the American coproducer should be consulted at least sixty days before shooting began. It did not specify, however, that consultation necessarily lead to compliance with Selznick's requests. Greene says that Reed played a waiting game.

Selznick arrived at conferences eager to reach binding agreements, complete with a stenographer to make a typescript of their conversation. To each of Selznick's demands Reed would say, "Yes, well, of course Graham and I will look into that," or "We'll take that into consideration." Selznick left them with forty pages of suggestions for changes. With Korda's complete approval Reed put the document in a drawer and never looked at it.[50]

The history of the making of *The Third Man* is riddled with cold-war and cinema politics. Even the date of the American première was changed three times because of a dispute between Selznick and Korda over distribution rights, from December, 1949, to early January, 1950, to late January, and finally to February. When *The Third Man* did arrive in New York, it had already won the Cannes Grand Prix and was well known to audiences in England, where it had opened in London five months earlier. Perhaps it should be noted that after rave reviews in London and New York the film was not well received in Vienna, where it was first shown on March 10, 1950. The Communist paper in that city claimed that it was "hot with anti-Russian propaganda and the philosophy of modern gangsters."[51]

Although Greene had wanted his story to remain outside the political arena, it is nevertheless the political ambience that makes the setting interesting and gives Lime credibility. What Reed and his photographer, Robert Krasker, made of Vienna is as much a part of war politics, of the nostalgia and fear that grow out of decay, as it is of the city's baroque architecture and haunting music. But Greene had wanted "reality . . . to be only the background to a fairy tale."[52] So, although the film is filled with violent deaths and disappearances that constantly remind us we are not in "the old Vienna with its Strauss music and its bogus easy charm,"[53] it has, nevertheless, a leisurely and somewhat sentimental Viennese tempo; the violence is kept at arm's length.

In the "Story," Greene had carefully controlled the tone through the point of view he chose. With Calloway as narrator we were removed from the story's violence by person and time; like *Went The Day Well?* the first *Third Man* came to us after the fact and filtered through the consciousness of a less likable character than the old vicar, but one we trusted by the time the most violent scenes occurred. On film this kind of control was difficult; even though a narrator's voice opens the movie, it is really the camera that tells us the story. Here Greene must further control the violence by having it occur offscreen. The children dying of Harry's penicillin are, therefore, hidden behind kindly nurses in the hospital in keeping with his directive: *"We take a rapid view of the six small beds, but we do not see the occupants, only the effect of horror on Martins's face."*[54] And Harry receives the coup de grâce in blackness at the far end of the tunnel. So even though there are many violent incidents, we are protected in this "fairy tale," as well as by point of view, by delicate camera work, by the constancy of Anna's and Martins's affection for Lime, and by the notes of Anton Karas's zither that continually fight back the reality of postwar Vienna.

Although Greene had associated a "signature tune" with Harry Lime from the beginning, Reed's late discovery of the zither player was a lucky find. The haunting notes create a sense of Lime's presence throughout the film and help maintain a balance between the fear and the romantic nostalgia that Greene had found in Vienna. On November 25, 1949, Selznick reported the music to be:

> rage of England and has already sold more record copies than any other record in entire history of record business in England. . . . It is one of those unpredictable, tremendous sensations that I cannot expect any of you to understand who have not been here. Entirely unrelated newspaper articles and editorials, even on politics, continually refer to it. Inevitably, this success will be repeated America if we are prepared for it. We should be able to make fortune out of this music.[55]

They did, indeed, make money from the zither Reed had so expertly used to support the tone of Greene's story. Although Karas's music was originally rejected by almost every publisher in London, when it was eventually recorded, Decca sold four million copies of the *Harry Lime Theme*. Selznick reported, " . . . even the big royalties . . . were nothing compared to the exploitation value of the song, which . . . did as much as any other factor . . . to put *The Third Man* into the language and to make this the most successful picture ever produced in England from a grossing standpoint, other than, conceivably, such a road show as *The Red Shoes*."[56] Whether the music contributed as greatly to *The Third Man*'s success as Selznick thought, it certainly made Anton Karas famous. He toured the nightclubs of Europe and America, played for the king and queen of England, and returned to Vienna to open a wine garden called "At the Sign of the Third Man."

The prestige of Cannes and the film's profit must have mollified

Selznick when he realized that Greene and Reed had not changed the direction of the film in the way he desired. Presumably the box-office receipts were more important than the political effect he had hoped to achieve, for he soon suggested that Greene might make another film for him, this time based on the life of Mary Magdalene. When Greene refused, Selznick offered another idea. "It will appeal to you as a Catholic," he told him. "You know how next year they have what's called The Holy Year in Rome. Well, I want to make a picture called *The Unholy Year*. It will show all the commercial rackets that go on, the crooks. . . . We'll shoot it in the Vatican." When Greene doubted they would give him permission for that, Selznick responded, "Oh sure they will. . . . You see, we'll write in one Good Character." The conversation, Greene says, reminds him of another, one he had with Sam Zimbalist, who wanted him to revise the end of a script for a remake of *Ben Hur* because he found "a kind of anti-climax after the Crucifixion."[57]

The story of turning *The Third Man* into film stands as a classic case history of what can happen when in the great arena of contemporary culture the armies of finance, art, and politics clash by night. Together with *The Fallen Idol*, it confirmed Greene's view that the cinema could produce works that were aesthetically as well as financially successful; alone, it proved how easily the equilibrium maintained in film making between art and high finance could be thrown off balance, for without Korda's devotion to Greene and Reed, Selznick might well have had his way, with who knows what aesthetic results. It was Greene's and Reed's artistic sense that made this film financially successful, and their ability to roll with Selznick's punches. If they were able to avoid what John Grierson, in describing the artistic limitations imposed on film makers by financers, called "their strait-jacket to the devil,"[58] it was by remaining faithful to what they felt to be artistically honest.

The Fallen Idol and *The Third Man* represent Greene and Reed at their cinematic best. The films are distinguished aesthetically by a harmonious combination of visual complexity and narrative simplicity. Ethically they are marked by the responsibility Greene felt that film makers should display. Both are fine examples of what he had in mind when he discussed the common poetic cinema, and both left critics and viewers alike eagerly awaiting the next Greene-Reed collaboration.

Richard Attenborough as Pinkie in *Brighton Rock*, 1947. Courtesy of The Museum of Modern Art, Film Stills Archive.

Bobby Henrey as Felipe in *The Fallen Idol*, 1948. Courtesy of The Museum of Modern Art, Film Stills Archive.

Sonia Dresdel as Mrs. Baines and Bobby Henrey as Felipe in *The Fallen Idol*, 1948. Courtesy of The Museum of Modern Art, Film Stills Archive.

Ralph Richardson as Baines and Bobby Henrey as Felipe in *The Fallen Idol*, 1948. Courtesy of The Museum of Modern Art, Film Stills Archive.

Joseph Cotten as Holly Martins in *The Third Man,* 1949. Courtesy of The Museum of Modern Art, Film Stills Archive.

Orson Welles as Harry Lime in *The Third Man*, 1949. Courtesy of The Museum of Modern Art, Film Stills Archive.

Orson Welles and Carol Reed on the set of *The Third Man*, 1949. Courtesy of Cahiers du Cinéma.

4

After the Grand Prix

The enormous success of *The Third Man* prompted several British newspapers to report the start of a third Greene-Reed venture. Greene had gone to Goslar, in the Harz Mountains, after completion of the movie because "Reed wanted to do a film about the British occupied and Russian occupied border in Germany." But this time his attempt to "dig something up was without success,"[1] and it was a decade, "a period of great unrest"[2] for him, before he and Reed collaborated again. From the Goslar trip there remains only "a film story which never came to anything."[3] Entitled *No Man's Land*, it is now among Greene's manuscripts in Austin, Texas.

The story has several obvious similarities to *The Third Man*. It is a thriller set in a politically divided area with borders that must be illegally crossed; the protagonist, Richard Brown, is searching for a dead relative; he is helped by Clara, a woman who has known the man and with whom Richard falls in love; and the moral tenor of the piece focuses on trust. In fact, the film story appears to be an attempt to reuse many of the thematic elements of *The Third Man*.

It begins in a restaurant, where its narrator, Redburn of the Boundary Inspection, has been watching Brown for many days. He warns Brown, when they later meet in a forest "a couple of miles east of Braunlage," not to lose his way, for they are close to the Russian zone, in no man's land, those three kilometers "with thick woods on either side, where the East and West Patrols work through the shadows, looking for smugglers or deserters."

The story cuts to the Russian side of the border, which Brown has illegally crossed from the British zone. There he meets Clara, "a beautiful, elegant woman," in a bread shop, where he frightens the shopkeeper by paying in Western marks and asking about a man he is trying to find. He passes another shop whose window is full of "holy junk" and stops to buy a medal. Here the old shopkeeper "looks at him then gives him the box of medals." In it he finds a cigarette case and under that a knife inscribed "R.B."

At a pilgrimage in front of a cave he hears Clara's voice tell him, "Kneel, kneel quickly," but cannot spot her. Instead he sees the police and leaves hurriedly. While eating his bread under a tree, he decides that if he is caught he will say he is "an English writer . . . writing a book about the Harz, its people, its superstitions." He is preparing to leave when he notices a man in a homburg watching him. As he gets up, his knife cuts into "a paper with numbers on it" that has been hidden in the loaf. He puts it back into a "piece of bread and puts the pellet into his ear."

The scene switches to an interrogation room and then to an eighteenth-century stone house, where he meets Clara again. Her fingers are "raw from cigarette burns." She asks who he is; he asks why she told him to kneel at the grotto; she says she will come to his room "when Strakov is asleep."

From Strakov, a Russian official, he learns that a week earlier an order had been given to stop pilgrimages to Eisleben because the government was "afraid of uranium mines." But although a spy has been recently caught there and executed, Strakov has not carried out the order to stop the pilgrimages because he believes that the place keeps people happy. He and Brown strike up an acquaintance.

Later Brown and Clara make love. He tells her he will return to the British zone to report the death of Kramer, the spy, who was also his half-brother. She tells him she gave Kramer away. "We should never have talked," he replies, "just made love till we got tired of it. Not talked." Greene interjects: "It was the stock situation of all melo-dramas; you were trapped by a woman."

The story proceeds quickly, crosscutting from Brown's and Stra-kov's conversations to Brown's and Clara's. Brown and Strakov discuss betrayal, in particular betrayal by women. Brown and Clara talk about Brown's departure. From their conversation we learn that Kramer has left a coded message about the Eisleben mines on microfilm in one of the wax candles in the grotto.

The lovers decide to secure the report and then return to the British zone. On leaving the house Clara accidentally awakens Strakov. He goes to Brown's room; Brown claims that he cannot sleep and would like to walk; Strakov engages him in a brief conversation about trust and allows Brown to walk alone in the yard. "I trust you," Strakov says. "Why? That's an odd thing to say. I have fallen in trust."

Clara and Brown meet in the forest and proceed to the grotto, where four candles are lighted. They watch a woman light the fifth one, the one with the microfilm in it. As Brown puts out the candle, Clara seizes it and takes it across the grotto to relight it. The man with the homburg reappears. Brown shoots him and seizes the film as Clara kneels praying over the dead man's body.

The story ends in the British zone with Brown relating the last details to Redburn; Clara has carried back three-quarters of a plaster rose from the Grotto; she and Brown are to be married. The narrator reports Strakov's death and tells us that the grotto has been de-molished. "After all," he says, "in the long run Brown had to discover that you can't love and not trust."

Aside from the plot and thematic similarities that *No Man's Land* shares with its predecessor, the story employs a first-person narrator, though Redburn, unlike Calloway, takes no part in the action. Before *The Third Man*, Greene had written some short stories in the first person but had not used the technique in a novel. "The Second Death" (1929), "A Day Saved" (1935), "Across the Bridge" (1938), "The Case for the Defence" (1939), "Alas, Poor Mailing" (1940) and "The Hint of an Explanation" (1948) were among them. Two films, *The New Britain* and *Went the Day Well?* had also been presented from this point of view. In 1951 he decided to try the form in *The End of the Affair*. "A moment comes in middle age," he explained, "when . . . [a novelist] feels that he no longer controls his method; he has become its prisoner. Then a long period of ennui sets in: it seems to him he has done everything before. . . . I had tried to escape from my prison by writing for the films, but *The Third Man* only beckoned me into another and more luxurious prison."[4]

Before returning from film to what he considered his "proper job," Greene read *Great Expectations* and was captivated by the ease with which Dickens used first-person narration. With this technique Greene thought he had found "an escape from the pattern, a method he had not tried." The first person offered the "obvious technical advantage" of ensuring against "any temptation to deviate, 'I' could only observe what 'I' observed." But he soon discovered that the technique was difficult and regretted pursuing it many times during the writing of *The End of the Affair*: "I had never previously had to struggle so hard to lend the narrative interest, . . . to vary the all important 'tone,' . . . but when I tried to analyze . . . [Dickens's] success, I felt like a colourblind man trying intellectually to distinguish one colour from another."[5]

First-person narration is not particularly cinematic, yet in *The Third Man* Greene had had no problem employing it. Colorblind or not, in the film he had used it to advantage. It helped ensure that the tone did not deviate from the frame of normality provided by the decent, if unimaginative, Major Calloway. Within that boundary Greene could maneuver through shades of love, loyalty, fear, and corruption while keeping the overall tale safe for the average viewer. But like the earlier first-person stories, *The Third Man* was a short work. A novel was more demanding, and Greene felt that from the first page of *The End of the Affair* when Bendrix wrote, "This is a record of hate far more than of love," the whole book would be "smoked dry like a fish" with his narrator's acrid comments.[6]

It was not until 1955 and *The Quiet American* that he dared use the first person again. By then he had spent three months of travel in Malaya in 1951 during the emergency as a correspondent for *Life*, and four winters in Vietnam from 1951 to 1955 reporting the French wars for the *Sunday Times* (London) and the *Figaro*. In 1953 he had gone to Kenya to report on the Mau Mau outbreak for the *Sunday Times*. It was no accident then, that in *The Quiet American* he choose a journalist for his narrator, a choice that "seemed to justify the use of *rapportage*."[7] Like Major Calloway in *The Third Man*, Fowler was a controlled, detached, almost toneless recorder of events. He began: "I thought in headlines. 'American official murdered in Saigon.'

Working on a newspaper one does not learn the way to break bad news, and even now I had to think of my paper."[8] Fowler was not as emotionally detached as Brown would be in *The Comedians* (1966), where the story is recorded with the soulless precision of a camera whose narrowness of vision produces deep irony and black humor. But like Brown and Greene's other first-person narrators, Henry in *Travels with My Aunt* (1969) and Jones in *Doctor Fischer of Geneva* (1980), Fowler could step back from his story to examine both his own role in it and the validity of his account. "Oh, I was right about the facts," he says, "but wasn't . . . [Pyle] right too to be young and mistaken, and wasn't he perhaps a better man for a girl to spend her life with?"[9]

Even the earlier Bendrix had done the same in *The End of the Affair*. "A story," he tells us, "has no beginning or end: arbitrarily one chooses that moment of experience from which to look back or from which to look ahead."[10] Like Calloway, who begins by reminding us that if we are to understand the strange, sad incident he is about to relate we will need some facts, Bendrix seems to have chosen his point of departure at random. He begins by focusing our attention on a particular place and set of conditions. "I say 'one chooses,' " he reflects, "with the inaccurate pride of a professional writer who—when he has been seriously noted at all—has been praised for his technical ability, but do I in fact of my own will *choose* that black wet January on the Common, in 1946, the sight of Henry Miles slanting across the wide river of rain, or did these images choose me?"[11]

Does a writer pick his point of departure, or is he, like a camera, confronted with a situation he cannot fail to record? In examining himself, Bendrix suspects that the images come first and that he, like Calloway, who claims to be unimaginative and to have reconstructed Lime's story from his files, is obliged to register them. As Fowler says: "My fellow journalists called themselves correspondents; I preferred the title of reporter. I wrote what I saw: I took no action."[12]

This method of narration bears no resemblance to the first-person accounts of Proust's memoir-novels, or Virginia Woolf's controlled stream of consciousness. Greene's is a rapportage approach that most often resembles film technique. He uses his narrator as a cinematographer does his camera, to switch the point of view. In juxtaposing the narrator's story with his examination of himself as an honest reporter, Greene finds a solution to the "colourblindness" he claims he experienced while writing *The End of the Affair*. Calloway could speak directly to the viewer from one vantage point and then fade into the story, allowing the camera to include him in its record of events; thus Greene's subsequent first-person narrators speak in the first person and then allow the point of view to shift away from their necessarily limited account to a broader view of the incidents of which they are a part.

When Brown tells us at the opening of *The Comedians*, "I was not involved, so far as I could tell, with either Jones or Smith, they were fellow passengers, that was all," he observes as a reporter or a cameraman would, aware that he records only one of an infinite number of possibilities. Then the point of view shifts, and he continues: "I had no idea of the *pompes funèbres* they were preparing for me in the parlours of Mr. Fernandez. If I had been told I would have laughed, as I laugh now on my better days."[13]

The method is similar to a cinematic jump cut except that the discrepancy in the image involves time, not distance. Unlike a jump cut, which is disturbing to watch because it breaks the visual continuity of a shot, this technique works extremely well on paper. It allows for an instantaneous shift in time and hence point of view. The objective Brown is swept up by forces beyond his control, as Bendrix suspected he had been when he was wondering whether the images chose him and as Fowler admits he is when he says, "I should have seen. . . . I might have saved all of us a lot of trouble, even Pyle, if I had realized the direction."[14]

This is a filmic, double-angled view. We get events of the story recorded by a seemingly nonparticipating objective observer juxtaposed with an account of his actions in the narrative. As Dominick Consolo observed in "Graham Greene: Style and Stylistics in Five Novels,"[15] this allows Greene to withhold information until he chooses to reveal it by making the entire account a reflection on itself, and gives the author many opportunities to add his own comments by shifting and arranging the individual sequences. It is very close to the way Calloway was employed—and indeed any first-person narrator *must* be employed—on the screen, where the camera always takes over from the speaker and includes him in the recorded events. On paper Calloway's authority is great, but on film he fades in and out of the story, appearing to be sometimes in control of the narrative and at other times merely one of the actors. The viewer of *The Third Man* is allowed a broader perspective of things because the camera shows him not only what Calloway thinks he ought to see but how Calloway looks in the action.

This loose, or what might be called cinematically shifting, first-person method that Greene adopted in his fiction is also similar to the style of his journalism in the years between *The Third Man* and *The Quiet American*. In his rapportage from Malaya, Kenya, and Indo-China he concentrated on particular incidents that caught his eye, adding to them by juxtaposing other points of view until the episodes became visual metaphors for the history playing itself out before him.

The march of the Gurkha patrol, "by the compass, and not by paths,"[16] in Malaya in 1951 exemplified the constancy of the unit. The fear of violent death—"photographs of a trunk from which the head had been severed remain long in memory"—the "flimsy lock on . . . [the settler's] bedroom door, the revolver by his bed and the vigilance of his dog"[17] showed the lonely lot of a farmer on the edge of the Aberdare or Kenya forest in 1953. The "ardent little scenes [that] took place in dug-outs" at Dien Bien Phu in January, 1954, the "woman suckling her baby beside a sentry under waiting hills," represented "the atmosphere heavy with doom."[18]

These images are like Eisensteinian close shots. They give the reader a greater understanding of the whole because they contain elements of the larger picture. In juxtaposing others with them, Greene broadens our view, often demanding empathy for individuals on both sides of any struggle. The method gives his rapportage a façade of objectivity, which he further encourages by pointing out that he is recording only his own impression of the situation.

Sometimes, he tells us, a journalist's point of view is so mis-directed that he entirely misses the event he has gone to witness. In Riga in the 1930s, Greene spent two hours walking in the streets around the Central Station and the Post Office while he waited for a train to Berlin. He was "charmed by the old droshky drivers with Tolstoy beards asleep over their bony horses, and by the prostitutes who might well have been plying their trade in Victorian London." In the morning he discovered that there had been a military coup d'état at the time he was walking. He read in the *Daily Telegraph* that the Post Office and the Central Station had been taken, but he "had seen only the old droshky drivers and the Victorian tarts."[19]

"The view of an outsider at a revolution is an odd and slanting one," he said, "rather like a pretentious camera-angle."[20] For accuracy the point of view must be shifted, the image qualified through juxtaposition. When a priest in Nyeri told him that the executed Africans he attended "die like angels, I don't often see Europeans die so well," Greene commented:

> When so many hundred times you have had to descend into the pit below the gallows to give the last rites to the broken-necked carrion lying there, each body becomes the body of an individual. You are in a different world from the courtroom at Githenguri with the rows of numbered black figures from which justice—with often insufficient means—tries to separate what we call the guilty from what we call the innocent.[21]

It is the point of view that makes all the difference. As the filmed Calloway moved in to comment and back to allow the story to flow around him, Greene the journalist moves in for a closer look, then back to see the individual image in context. In juxtaposing the various angles of vision he gives both his rapportage, where he himself is chronicler, and those novels in which he employs a first person narrator authenticity and tone. This "looseness" in the point of view, necessitated by the camera in *The Third Man*, is what adds that spectrum of color Greene was looking for in *The End of the Affair* and his later novels written in the first person. It is a method that provides the intimacy and believability of the first-person point of view without the limited field of vision usually associated with its use. Greene is able to lend objectivity to his story by making his narrator examine himself from outside as well as from within. And he gives breadth to his writing by juxtaposing several of his narrator's accounts from different angles at different times.

In this instance the methods of film and novel seem to have merged. But the benefit went only to Greene's fiction. His sketch for *No Man's Land* was unpromising, and the films he made during the 1950s were disappointing. "Two halcyon years with Carol Reed," he reflected, "and I began to believe that I was learning the craft, . . . but it was an illusion. No craft had been learnt, there had only been the luck of working with a fine director who could control his actors and his production."[22] While he waited for the chance to work with Reed again, he continued to make films with other directors. He wrote scripts, sometimes following the pattern of *The Third Man*, he adapted Shaw's *Saint Joan*, he coproduced two movies, and he stood back and allowed other film makers to try their hand at transforming his work.

The first of his novels to be adapted after *The Third Man* was *The Heart of the Matter* (1953). It was directed by George More O'Ferrall. Trevor Howard played Scobie; Elizabeth Allan, Louise; and Maria Schell, Helen. The major change that scriptwriter Ian Dalrymple made in Greene's novel was in the ending, which was altered because of censorship. "In most countries," O'Ferrall explained, "censors would not allow a film in which a hero committed suicide."[23] Instead the film makers have Scobie take his gun and drive away from the house intending to shoot himself because he "wants to stop hurting people." As he parks, he sees a boy beaten up by several men and goes to help him. In the struggle he is shot with his own gun and dies, a smile on his face, muttering to Ali: "Going on trek. Tell Mrs., God made it all right for her."

Greene tried to persuade the film makers to leave the suicide in and even figured out a way to do it by showing Trevor Howard's hand writing a suicide note with the gun lying beside the paper. That way Scobie could be called away on police business and shot with the intention of suicide in mind. But O'Ferrall went ahead with Dalrymple's ending, which, if less effective, carried something of the same intention on the screen.

English reviews argued that the new conclusion weakened the story. The film was nevertheless entered at Cannes in 1953. It failed to win an award but later became notorious when it was banned in Singapore and Malaya because it depicted an assistant commissioner of police in a British Colonial Territory in "an unfavourable manner."[24] Greene responded with "puzzled amusement." "Surely," he said, "it was Mad Hatter policy to ban a serious British film, while admitting 'American trash.' "[25]

A year later he decided to leave his familiar role as scriptwriter and become involved in producing *The Stranger's Hand*. There may be a solution to the mistreatment of one's work, he thought, "if the author takes a hand in the production."[26] The project began when John Stafford asked him to write a story set in Italy. Mario Soldati— whom Greene many years later used as a model for Mario, Mr. Visconti's son, in *Travels with My Aunt*—was to direct. In 1949, signing himself as M. Wilkinson, Greene had won a *New Statesman* competition for writing the best opening to a new novel by any of the English novelists named Green(e). At the time he had no idea how the story would go on, but in 1954 he used the paragraph to begin *The Stranger's Hand*. He wrote two drafts for the film but was "busy with other things"[27] and turned the script over to Guy Elmes and Georgio Bassani. He was nevertheless on location in Venice during some of the shooting and did much of the spot casting himself.

Like *No Man's Land*, this film often resembles *The Third Man*. "There is another disappearance in a European city near the Iron Curtain, Trevor Howard is again the major in British Intelligence, Alida Valli is once more the lonely refugee, and this time Richard Basehart is the American boyfriend. The villain of the title is also a compound of evil and regret and other qualities."[28] With the addition of Roger Court, a young schoolboy on holiday who has arrived in Venice to meet his father, the story takes on echoes of *The Fallen Idol* as well.

The first draft of Greene's story remains unfinished.[29] It begins with Aunt Rose placing Roger Court in the care of a stewardess at the Rome airport. The boy, who no longer lives with his mother, is to meet his father, a security officer on leave from Trieste, in Venice.

When he arrives at the hotel, he is given a letter saying that his father will arrive at eight o'clock to dine with him. The boy goes to sleep but is awakened by a telephone call from a man saying he is Major Court; he has just left the train and will arrive in half an hour. Roger does not recognize his father's voice but nevertheless watches at his window in the hope that he will come. After some time the boy goes back to sleep.

When he awakens he discovers that the major has not arrived. The police are sent for, and the search begins. Roger is told that his father will arrive on the American train in a few hours. "No," the boy insists, "he came last night. I think he's been murdered." However, since Roger has not spoken to or seen his father for three years, it is difficult for the commissioner to ascertain whether the conversation the boy had the previous night was, in fact, with him. Phone calls are made, but there is no indication that Roger's father was on the train. In looking for his aunt's French address, the child finds a magic formula for making gunpowder in his pocket, and he and the commissioner speculate about this.

Eventually Roger walks about Venice trying to remember what his father looked like. He gets lost and peers into the doorway of a doctor's house, but when the doctor comes out and says he will take him home, the child becomes suspicious and lies, saying that he is staying at the Grand Hotel with his mother. They have ice cream together, and Roger changes his story, admitting that he is staying at the Europa. Roger asks whether the doctor's patients die, and during the ensuing discussion the doctor wins his confidence. Roger confesses that his mother is not with him and that he has lost his father.

Returning to the hotel, he finds that his father has still not arrived and that he himself has been moved to a smaller room. He goes to a café, where he is befriended by Roberto, one of the waiters. From the café window he sees his father and, running outside, sees him again but ultimately loses him in the crowd. He tells Roberto what has happened and asks him to pray for the major. The first draft ends with the waiter saying, "I am not a Roman Catholic."

In revision Greene's story begins the same way, but after Roger receives the letter and phone call and goes back to sleep, it cuts to a brief scene in which we meet Major Court. He and a doctor are discussing Pascal. The major says he does not know Venice and is given some medicine.

The following morning Roger is taken by the British consul to the police station, where he insists that he has spoken to his father on the telephone. In searching the docks with the police, he sees the doctor who he says has given him ice cream. The police try to verify the story by questioning the doctor's patients but find nothing. They are, however, suspicious and decide to investigate further.

Roger meets Roberto, and they talk of the possibility that Major Court (now a policeman from Trieste) is dead. They "figure out where he is" and together find the boy's father. He has been speared. The boy looks at his face and says, "I would hardly have known him." The story ends with the police commenting that they should have begun their search twenty-four hours earlier.

Greene's story is rather sketchy, but it provided the situation and major characters for the script. In the film the boy arrives in Venice as in the treatment. Major Court disappears en route to the hotel when he follows a familiar face in the crowd. It is Roberta (the hotel receptionist) who helps Roger and who calls the police. The doctor, Vivaldi, is an enemy agent; he drugs Major Court and keeps him among his patients so that upon examination neither the police nor Roger can recognize him. Later, when the boy is with Roberta and her American boyfriend, Joe Hamstringer, he realizes he has seen the major and returns to the doctor's flat but finds it empty.

Roberta and Roger go to the police, while Joe goes to the harbor

and sets fire to a foreign ship on which he thinks the major is being
kept prisoner. He wants to attract the attention of the police, who
have not believed Roger, and give them occasion to board a foreign
vessel. Finally the boat is searched, and Roger's father is rescued.
Vivaldi dies in the struggle.

Greene has happy memories of the filming of *The Stranger's Hand*:
"days at Venice drinking grappa with Mario Soldati, running races
down the Giudecca with Trevor Howard, the friendliness of the
Italian crew." But there were also problems. "We had to take a tea
break or pay the Italians overtime; but the Italians didn't want tea;
and the English complained when they couldn't get eggs and bacon
for breakfast."[30] The venture he undertook in the hope of gaining
tighter control of his work led him to another conclusion: that "to be
a co-producer is no job for a writer. One becomes involved with the
producer's monetary troubles."[31]

But what exactly did he do in this film to maintain the purity of his
story? The movie appears as "Graham Greene's," the production is
listed "in association with" him, and yet "when we look further his
share remains unspecified. He didn't write the screenplay or direct.
His hand is there, in characters, story, setting, and dialogue; but it
is," as the *New Statesman*'s reviewer noted, "one might say—a stranger's hand."[32]

Critical opinion of the film varied. Leonard Mosley called the
movie "a curious, uneven, and yet often compelling film,. . . not a
great film . . . but a fascinating one."[33] William Whitebait said that
it looked "remarkably well on the screen."[34] C. Ray wrote that "the
plot limps, . . . but there is evidence in almost every foot of an artist
having been at work, even if at one remove or more."[35] The *Glasgow
Herald*'s reviewer concluded: " . . . there is no Carol Reed, . . . there is
no zither either, . . . [and] Richard O'Sullivan . . . is no Bobby
Henrey."[36] But if *The Stranger's Hand*, whose mood and method were
reminiscent of *The Third Man* and *The Fallen Idol*, lacked the impact
of the former and the poignancy of the latter, it was well enough
received for Greene to write a screenplay for *Loser Takes All* and to try
his hand again at coproduction two years later.

Here, "for the first time—and I think the last," he says, he "drew a
principal character from life. Dreuther, the business tycoon, . . . is
undeniably Alexander Korda. . . . the story . . . is soaked in memories
of Alex. . . . I have . . . used scraps of his dialogue. . . . He even
provided me with the plot."[37]

It all began when Greene and a friend were to meet Korda at the Hôtel Grande Bretagne in Athens and go with him for a cruise in Korda's yacht, the *Elsewhere*. When Greene arrived at the "very expensive" hotel, with "very little money," he found "no Korda and no message. . . . The first day we were alone we were extravagant, but waking a second morning with no news of the boat, we had to be careful . . . which meant being more extravagant: all our meals in the hotel rather than in a cheap café; in place of a taxi an expensive hotel car which could be put on the bill. . . . Well, Alex like Dreuther did eventually turn up in time to pay our 'honeymoon' bill, and the story of *Loser Takes All* had been born."[38]

It was written in the Hôtel de Paris in Monte Carlo, where Greene followed a strict routine of writing, eating, and gambling. By the end of his stay he had made a profit of four pounds: he never discovered a system like that of his protagonist Bertrand. The story was sold to *Picture Post* and serialized in August and September, 1954. Ken Annakin, the film's director, and John Stafford, its producer, heard about the piece over dinner one evening and wanted to film it. They did not think Greene would let them have it because it "was too uncharacteristic" of his work.[39] But he wanted another chance to coproduce, for which he was never given film credit, and this time he decided to write the screenplay, for which he was paid £15,000.

Greene says he could see the film was "not good" long before it was completed but was unable to stop its production because Stafford "hadn't much money" and needed to complete the picture.[40] Again his attempt to govern the production seems to have failed. "The film," he admits, "proved a disaster of miscasting, with a middle-aged actress [Glynis Johns] as the twenty-year-old heroine, a romantic Italian star as the unromantic English accountant [Rossano Brazzi], and Robert Morley playing Robert Morley. . . . Alex had his little revenge (he must certainly have recognized himself as Dreuther) by refusing permission for Alec Guinness, who was under contract to him, to play the part."[41]

Critics confirmed Greene's judgment. They found *Loser Takes All* "sporadically amusing"[42] but "vulgar"[43] and "uninventive."[44] "Had I not seen it in writing," one reviewer commented, "I would find it hard to believe that such feeble dialogue . . . could be his."[45] But then it was not, for Greene claims that he watched his screenplay ruined when it was turned into the shooting script.

There were so many factors involved in getting one's work safely onto the screen. Was the answer to direct? Greene says that he gained as much film knowledge as he could for use in his criticism and scripts, but without the intention of using it to direct. "A good director like Carol Reed is in control; but the cameraman often takes over. I didn't think I ever had the expertise to do it."[46] And so, although he once admitted to going "further along this road in a film which shall be nameless,"[47] after *The Stranger's Hand* and *Loser Takes All* he returned to his usual role as scriptwriter and kept hoping for another chance to work with Reed.

In 1955, between these two adventures in coproduction, *The End of the Affair* was released. Greene went to the United States in 1952 to receive the Catholic Literary Award for the novel and was reported to be going to "Hollywood to write the script for *The End of the Affair*. . . . Every actress of note in the film city is angling for the starring role of Sarah Miles. Greer Garson wants to play it: so does Loretta Young,"[48] Roderick Mann wrote in the *Daily Graphic*.

But Greene's entry visa was held up. Under the McCarran Act he had become "a prohibited immigrant to the United States. At the age of nineteen for the fun of the thing," he says, "I had joined the Communist Party in Oxford as a probationary member and during my short stay with them contributed four sixpenny stamps monthly to the Party's funds." Naïvely he disclosed this story to a *Time* correspondent after a friend, the first secretary of the American embassy in Brussels, told him "the State Department were anxious for cases which would expose the absurdity of the Act. . . . The plastic curtain fell immediately."[49]

Later in the year when Charlie Chaplin was refused reentry to the United States after leaving for Europe to attend the premier of *Limelight*, Greene took the opportunity to attack the act in an open letter, "Dear Mr. Chaplin," published in the *New Republic* in October, 1952. In it he suggested that Chaplin make a film in which the Tramp be summoned from obscurity by the House Un-American Activities Committee and ended by saying that in attacking Chaplin "the witch-hunters have emphasized that this is no national matter. Intolerance in any country wounds freedom throughout the world."[50]

The End of the Affair went on without him under the direction of Edward Dmytryk, and with a script by Lenore Coffee. Unlike the novel, the story followed a chronological sequence of events. Dmytryk first arranged the scenes as they were in the book, which Greene had "ingeniously constructed to avoid the tedium of the time sequence."[51] But the film's producers thought a chronological order would be more understandable to the average viewer, and so, although both Dmytryk and Greene preferred the original editing, the film was respliced. But, as in the novel, Bendrix (played by Van Johnson) narrates the story until Sarah's (Deborah Kerr) diary is produced; she then takes over to tell why their affair has ended.

This first-person technique, which was becoming common in Greene's films, was very effective. By switching from Bendrix's account to Sarah's through the device of the diary, the viewer was able to observe the end of the affair from both points of view. Yet the film was strangely unreal. Perhaps, the *Spectator*'s reviewer suggested, "the agonies of the soul are not photogenic."[52]

Dmytryk foresaw that there might be a problem with the miracles and left them out. If you "show them on the screen," he said, "you seem to be insisting that the audience believe that they really happened." They were not important. What was important was Sarah's belief that her prayer had kept Bendrix alive, a belief that changed her life. Dmytryk felt that the miracles were peripheral to this.[53] In the collected edition of the novel Greene decided to change them as well. He said:

> I had been cheating—cheating myself, cheating the reader. . . . The incident of the atheist Smythe's strawberry mark (apparently cured by Sarah after her death) should have no place in the book; every so-called miracle, like the curing of Parkis's boy, ought to have had a completely natural explanation. The coincidences should have continued over the years, battering the mind of Bendrix, forcing on him a reluctant doubt of his own atheism. . . . but I had spurred myself too quickly to the end, . . . so . . . in a later edition I tried to return nearer to my original intention. Smythe's strawberry mark gave place to a disease of the skin which might have had a nervous origin and be susceptible to faith healing.

Sarah's secret baptism remained because it was "not necessarily in the realm of 'magic.' "[54] Dmytryk left it in too but tempered it with Bendrix's statement that "you can't mark a child for life by a splash of water and a few murmured words."

In 1957 four further films based on Greene's fiction were released. *Across the Bridge* was adapted by Guy Elmes and Dennis Freeman from a story of the same name written in 1938. Aside from the title, the setting, the dog (Rover in the story and Dolores in the film), and the death of the protagonist as he tries to save his pet, the movie bears very little similarity to the original. The script writers even turned Calloway, Greene's British hero, into Schaffner, a German.

The Quiet American was more disturbing. It so badly distorted Greene's work that he claimed it made "the most extreme changes I have seen in any book of mine. . . . One could almost believe that the film was made deliberately to attack the book and the author."[55] Britain's film critics rose to the occasion. Nina Hibbin called it "doctored Greene";[56] Leonard Mosley, a "whitewash job";[57] Dilys Powell, an "assassination."[58]

Joseph L. Mankiewicz, who wrote the script and directed the film, offered no defense for what he had done to the novel. "I've often wanted to do a picture about one of those ice-blooded intellectuals," he told Arthur Knight, "whose intellectualism is really just a mask for completely irrational passion. . . . Fowler, I felt, was such a character." His only worry was "how the public is going to take my *Quiet American*. How many of them ever heard of Michael Redgrave [Fowler]? And what will Audie Murphy [Pyle] fans think when they find their hero dead in the mud in the very first shot?"[59]

To please his United States box office, Mankiewicz made the American wise and the Englishman the dupe of the Communists. Michael Redgrave has quoted Greene as saying that he was "very angry, indeed," about the political dishonesty of the film. "He almost had to be forcibly held down when he heard that United Artists had given all proceeds from the Washington premiere . . . to an aid-for-Vietnam drive. He was even more annoyed when he heard that he had been allotted a seat beside Vietnam's ambassador at the coming London première."[60] Greene closed the issue with admirable restraint: "The book was based on a closer knowledge of the Indo-China war than the American director possessed and I am vain enough to believe that the book will survive a few years longer than Mr. Mankiewicz's incoherent picture."[61]

Short Cut to Hell, James Cagney's remake of *This Gun for Hire* also appeared, as did Greene's adaptation of Bernard Shaw's *Saint Joan*. "The critics will say another deplorable adaptation," Greene thought, "though I would myself defend the script for retaining, however rearranged, Shaw's epilogue and for keeping a sense of responsibility to the author while reducing a play of three-and-a-half hours to a film of less than two hours."[62]

The dialogue, indeed the whole film, *is* remarkably faithful to Shaw's play. But the story is told "in a little different continuity in order to adjust it," Otto Preminger, the director and producer, said, "to adapt it to the picture medium."[63] The major change was moving the epilogue to the beginning, so that the film opens in the king's bedroom with Joan telling Charles that he is dreaming and Charles reminiscing about Joan's ability to have her way with the "Archbishop, with me, with all of us. It was a miracle," he says. "No, Charlie," she replies, "it was only a matter of eggs," and we are immediately taken back to the Baudricourt scene that opens Shaw's play.

The film continues as the original until the coronation scene. Between it and the trial Greene introduces Warwick so that the viewer will know he has bought Joan from his allies and, not wishing to be responsible for her death, has turned her over to the group of French clergy who believe her a heretic. Finally Greene uses Warwick to tell of the annulment of Joan's sentence in 1456 and her beatification and canonization in 1909 and 1919.

Greene thought these changes a good idea, especially using the epilogue as a prologue. Yet several of them alter Shaw's view of Joan's trial, which clearly holds the entire church responsible for her execution; the film script supports the church and places the blame solely on her judges. For example, following the acceptance of Joan's recantation, Greene has de Stogumber rush out of the room to tell Warwick what has happened. In the added dialogue de Stogumber begs Warwick not to hold the church responsible but rather to blame only those priests who conducted the trial. Warwick takes the news calmly, saying, "I thought it probable," and assures the chaplain that Joan will die before the pope hears of the matter. In this way Greene removes the culpability of the church.

He also reinterprets the incident in Shaw's scene 2, where Foul Mouthed Frank, "the only man in Touraine who could beat . . . [La Hire] at swearing, was told by a soldier that he shouldn't use such language when he was at the point of death."[64] Shaw's Frank falls into a well and drowns. Greene's Frank, who is lecherous rather than drunken, seizes Joan. She says that he will soon die, which he does instantly, with his hands raised to heaven. Greene uses this "miracle" to foreshadow her sanctity and remove responsibility from the church for what will happen to her: since she is a saint, the church will eventually recognize her and separate itself from her executioners.

Although in other ways faithful to Shaw, the film was a failure aesthetically and a box-office flop. The role of Joan was beyond Jean Seburg, who, Greene commented, "couldn't act. She was tested only for monologue," and when confronted with the impressive cast that Preminger had built around her, which included John Gielgud as Warwick, Richard Widmark as Charles, Richard Todd as Dunois, Bernard Miles as the Executioner, and Anton Walbrook as Cauchon, "she continued to talk only to herself."[65]

Preminger launched a worldwide search to find his heroine, a search that included 3,000 auditions and cost £50,000. He chose her from the 18,000 girls who applied to be screen-tested, for her "sincerity and honesty," those qualities he felt necessary for the part. He wanted a young, unknown actress for what he considered "one of the greatest plays ever written." He also wanted the "picture deliberately in black-and-white, on the normal screen, because I want to put the emphasis on people, on characterizations, on emotions, and on the words by Bernard Shaw."[66]

Given his expressed desire to adapt Shaw faithfully, it is surprising that Preminger did not avail himself of the screenplay Shaw had written for *Saint Joan* between 1934 and 1936. The script was never filmed because Shaw dropped the project when the Hollywood censorship bureau demanded what he considered absurd changes. The Hays Office included "a body called the Catholic Action, professing, on what authority I know not, to be a Roman Catholic doctrinal censorship," Shaw reported. It demanded:

> . . . that Cauchon's "The Church cannot take life" be changed to "The Church does not wish death"; that such words as "damned," "St. Denis," and "infernal" be deleted; that the scene wherein Joan is "spared the customary torture . . . be omitted from the film, not because it is not true, but because it is 'essentially damaging.' " Because of the censorship, Elisabeth Bergner, who was to play Joan, "is to be seen everywhere on the screen as Catherine of Russia, Empress of Freethinkers and Free Lovers, but may not make the world fall in love with a Catholic saint as she did when she created the part of Joan in Protestant Berlin when my play was new."[67]

If Shaw's script had been changed in accordance with these and the

Hays Office's other proposed deletions, the church would have appeared somewhat less culpable, which is in fact the result of Greene's adaptation.

Both he and Preminger claim they did not know the Shaw script existed.[68] But this is odd on Greene's part. As critic and scriptwriter he was very sensitive to censorship, rarely missing an occasion to expose its results. When Shaw's film script was finished, Greene was movie reviewer for the *Spectator*, and the argument with the Hays Office was far from silent; the controversy was followed in the press, the *New York Times* publishing a letter from Shaw on September 14, 1936, in which he openly attacked the censor's judgments.

Greene allows only that "Preminger was insistent . . . I do the screenplay, and I did have six weeks blank, so I acceded. Shaw is not a sacred name to me. I didn't mind adapting his work."[69] Perhaps if one goes on record as being interested in "keeping a sense of responsibility to the author" and then changes his Protestant Joan into a Catholic one, it is preferable not to remember the argument with the Hays Office. But what then does one expect from adaptations? Today Greene says, "Only that they should be a true reflection of character. I don't mind if the plot's changed as long as the characters come out whole. In general I don't think adaptations are a good idea, though Dickens has been done well."[70] In Preminger's film Shaw was not, and after it, Greene gave up adapting other writers' work for good.

He also began to despair of writing for the cinema altogether. He claims that the 1950s were a period of "great torment" for him during which film work became "drudgery" that produced unsuccessful movies and "manic depression reached its height":

> There had been, of course, moments of great interest in learning the new craft of film writing, but so often the excitement of creation was confined to the preliminary idea, sketched at a dinner table, and lost again in the many rewritings, the first, second and third treatment, the first, second and third script. The screen is not there . . . on which to test an idea; nor is there a stage from which the author can hear his lines brought to life or exhibited in their deadness. When the lines are at last spoken on the studio-floor the author is not there to criticize and alter. Another hand (. . . perhaps more easily controlled by the director) plays with his work. . . . A film studio—when you are allowed to penetrate it—has the callow comradeship of a great factory: signs, lights, clappers, cranes, and

behind all the façade of Christian names . . . the hierarchy of canvas chairs.

And so he took a rest from both novels and film in "writing plays which were produced." Comparing the experience with movie work he wrote that the theater was different:

> I had not anticipated the warmth, the amusement, and comradeship. . . .
> Above all I had not realized that the act of creation, as with the novel,
> would continue so long after the first draft of the play was completed,
> that it would extend through rehearsals and through the opening weeks
> of the tour. It is for the act of creation that one lives, and . . . there had
> been the excitement of acceptance, the excitement and frustrations of
> casting, the grim interest of auditions when every line became more
> leaden, the first reading with the complete cast, the conferences and
> changes over coffee, the delight of working with players interested not
> only in their own parts but in the play as a whole. . . .[71]

Only in *The Fallen Idol* and *The Third Man* had Greene been close enough to the center of film making to experience any of these satisfactions. His ventures into production had proved fruitless, and the many films with which his name was associated in the 1950s were undistinguished. It is perfectly understandable then that after ten unsatisfactory years he jumped at the opportunity to work again with Carol Reed. This came in November, 1958. Although Alfred Hitchcock, whose films Greene as a critic had never liked, had been trying to buy *Our Man in Havana* for several months, Greene sold the rights to Reed and left with him for Cuba the same night.[72]

This is an example of a novel that began as an idea for a movie. Soon after the war Alberto Cavalcanti asked Greene to write a film for him. Greene thought of a Secret Service comedy based on the knowledge he had gained during the war of the German Abwehr activity in Portugal. When he returned from Freetown, he had been appointed to Kim Philby's subsection of the Secret Service, which dealt with counterespionage in the Iberian Peninsula. His responsibility was Portugal. "There," he says, "those Abwehr officers who had not been suborned already by our own service spent much of their time sending home completely erroneous reports based on information received from imaginary agents. It was a paying game, especially when expenses and bonuses were added to the cypher's salary, and a safe one."

The story's first version "was an outline on a single sheet of paper,

. . . laid in 1938, in Tallinn, the capital of Estonia. . . . The English agent had nothing at this stage . . . to do with vacuum cleaners, and it was the extravagance of his wife and not his daughter which led him to cheat his service. He was a more besotted character than Wormold . . . and less innocent. As the 1939 war approached, his enemies, like Wormold's, began to treat him seriously—the local police too. The incident on the misused micro-photographs was already in this draft."

Since the plot poked fun at the British Secret Service, Cavalcanti decided they ought to have the project cleared by the censor before arranging for production. "He was told that no certificate could be issued," Greene says. "At least that was the story he told me. Perhaps he invented an excuse because he was not enamoured of the subject." But the idea remained in Greene's mind, and during the several visits he made to Havana in the 1950s, he came to realize he had been

> planning the wrong situation and placing it at the wrong period. The shadows in 1938 of the war to come had been too dark for comedy; the reader could feel no sympathy for a man who was cheating his country in Hitler's day for the sake of an extravagant wife. But in fantastic Havana, among the absurdities of the Cold War (for who can accept the survival of Western capitalism as a great cause?) there was a situation allowably comic, all the more if I changed the wife into a daughter.[73]

Our Man in Havana was published in 1958, and Greene turned it into a film script the same year. He and Reed shared a suite in a Brighton hotel. "I woke early," he recalls, "while Reed slept, worked, gave what I had written to our secretary to type. . . . We spent afternoon and evening in the sitting room discussing the day's work. There were many arguments and therefore much tension. This was resolved either by a compromise or by a new idea which arose out of our quarrel."[74]

At first it was thought necessary to film the story in Cádiz, so close was its shooting date to the time Castro took power in Cuba. But an arrangement was made through William Graf, Columbia Pictures' London production executive, for the crew to go to Havana, and the rushes were flown daily to editor Bert Bates in London, who in turn wired the results back to Reed. On location the British personnel were matched by Cuban standbys and Clara Martínez, a member of the Film Division of the Cuban Ministry of the Interior, was assigned to the team. Her job, Reed said, was "to make sure that our story . . .

shows just what a police state it was [during Batista's regime]."[75] She requested "about 39 script changes" most of which had to do with the character of Captain Segura, a thinly disguised version of Batista's notoriously sadistic police chief, Colonel Ventura. The government, Greene explained, thought Segura too nice. They "would have liked the police chief to be a real 'heavy' but how can you have such a bad villain in what's meant to be a light comedy?"[76]

The screenplay is interesting to study in manuscript, for, like Greene's adaptation of Shaw's *Saint Joan*, it incorporates actual pages of the novel that have been pasted onto type sheets and altered only slightly by pen. One such sequence is the European Traders' lunch. The novel's text from just before the sequence in which Hasselbacher warns Wormold not to go to lunch to where Wormold tells Beatrice: "I'm not under the table. I have come back victorious," is inserted into the script. Only minimal changes have been made until the poisoned whisky is handed to Wormold (Alec Guinness). From there the text is shortened, and Carter's stuttered words are changed to "H-h-happy days." These are interjected into the beginning of Wormold's speech, which is trimmed. The talk about Hasselbacher is removed. Wormold gives his whisky to the dog exactly as in the original, but the dog dies and is carried out the service door more quickly. Wormold exits immediately afterward, and the sequence dissolves into a crowded street. Segura is seen, and Hasselbacher's body. Police are everywhere.

All that seemed necessary to alter in these ten pages was to exclude monologue and hurry things slightly. Greene's prose had a precise simplicity and a fluency of movement appropriate to the film. Here, as in many other scenes, he was able to turn his novel almost directly into a screenplay simply by adding camera and set directions.

The larger changes he made to the original increase the situational comedy in the story by making visual those sections of the novel that contain comic possibilities. In the original, for example, Wormold finds

> a list of Country Club members in Milly's room. He knew where to look for it, between the latest volume of *Horsewoman's Year Book* and a novel called *White Mare* by Miss 'Pony' Traggers. He had joined the Country Club to find suitable agents, and here they all were in double column, over twenty pages of them. His eye caught an Anglo-Saxon name— Vincent C. Parkman. . . . By the time he sat down to encode he had

chosen two other names—an Engineer Cifuentes and a Professor Luis Sanchez.[77]

On film this is expanded into the immensely funny sequence in which Wormold, in imitation of Hawthorne's method of recruiting him, tries to lure Cifuentes into the washroom at the Havana Club, only to be followed there by Captain Segura. Similarly, Wormold's dream about recruiting Teresa, the girl who dances naked at the Shanghai Club in the novel, is acted out. Reed splits his screen to give us a picture of Wormold typing his report on one side and his fantasy about the stripper on the other.

These changes increase the film's buffoonery while maintaining the tone of the novel, in which Wormold himself is not funny though he is involved in situations that are. But in lightening *Our Man in Havana*, Greene created a less complicated Wormold, and perhaps that is where the problem lies.

In the novel the mood shifts from funny to serious to romantic as a parallel is drawn between Wormold and the novelist. Our attention is constantly focused on the fact that Wormold is like a writer in recognizing individuality, in playing at being in the Secret Service, and in inventing situations. He tries to be a clown in the classical tradition, to invent and play a serious role behind a comic mask. "We should all be clowns," he tells Milly, and then comments:

> The cruel come and go like cities and thrones and powers, leaving their ruins behind them. They had no permanence. But the clown whom he had seen last year with Milly at the circus—that clown was permanent, for his act never changed. That was the way to live; the clown was unaffected by the vagaries of public men and the enormous discoveries of the great.[78]

But cruelty does exist, and the world will not allow Wormold to play. It catches him. Like a novel that may have begun as an unlikely fairy story and ended in another vein, his creation takes on its own colors in becoming real. Wormold is trapped with the characters he has imagined in the world he has created, and when this happens, he seems to have failed as a clown.

Yet as with many of Greene's other characters, what seems to be Wormold's vices are really his virtues. The curiosity he has about other people and the absolute respect he holds for their individuality produce the situation he finds himself in when Dr. Hasselbacher is killed. These qualities also get him out of it. When Carter confesses, the man becomes real to Wormold, and our protagonist is prevented from killing except in self defense. Later, in telling of his hoax to the London office, Wormold's novelist's honesty obliges him "to ridicule himself in ridiculing human nature."[79] He thus passes untouched through both experiences, and the novel ends lightly.

The likeness between Wormold and a writer facilitates the change in mood from spy spoof to something more serious and back again. But in increasing the situational comedy of the story during its film adaptation, Greene removed the novel's emphasis on this parallel. It is only hinted at in the movie, and even then in scenes that become little more than awkward interruptions to the flow of the narrative. So the clown sequence, which in the novel carries so much of Wormold's attitude to life, is rendered comically on film. Because we have not associated Wormold with the creative act, the novel's bittersweet lines are out of place when delivered by Alec Guinness, a wash basin on his head, to Milly, who sits giggling in girlish pajamas. And this scene is better integrated than some. There is no precedent for the tenderness suggested in the confession Wormold makes to Beatrice on the balcony of his apartment as there is in the novel. There is a similar lack of credibility in some of the conversations he has with Dr. Hasselbacher.

When the film was released, reviewers felt that Guinness was responsible for what they called a problem of mood. He gives a "faceless and dull performance,"[80] one said. "He tries to smooth over the jolt from fantasy to flesh and blood by himself staying the same," another suggested, "and the incongruity between his own constancy and his violently altered circumstances serves only to accentuate the break in mood."[81] But if we compare the novel with the film, we see that these sentiments, reiterated more recently by Gene Phillips after Alec Guinness told him, "I don't think that I ever quite caught the character of Wormold,"[82] do not get at the root of the problem.

When in the novel Wormold becomes pensive and ruminates about life, what he says is built up to and supported by the connection between what is happening to him and the creative act. For example, when he and Beatrice return to his house after leaving Dr. Hasselbacher's flat, where they have learned of Raul's accident, they are frightened by a noise upstairs. On film the sequence is reduced considerably and followed by Cifuentes being dropped, tied and gagged, from a car into the street outside their door. It provides tension for a brief period and in connecting Dr. Hasselbacher's telephone conversation with the dumping of Cifuentes indicates that things are getting out of hand.

In the novel reality takes on another dimension when Wormold tells us he is more frightened than Beatrice is. "Can we write human beings into existence?" he asks. "And what sort of existence? Had Shakespeare listened to the news of Duncan's death in a tavern or heard the knocking on his own bedroom door after he had finished the writing of Macbeth? . . . [Wormold] thought he was afraid only of his own imaginary characters, not of a living person who could creak a board."[83]

The weight of importance here is on the imaginary, not the reality that a camera picks up. It is reduced in the novel before the end of the scene to "the *Boy's Own Paper* world." When imagined reality becomes visible and takes on shades of the *Sunday Mirror*, Wormold denies its validity. " 'You advised me to lie and I lied,' " he insists. " 'They were nothing but inventions, Hasselbacher.' . . . 'Then you invented . . . too well,' " the doctor returns, and the two continue their conversation, Hasselbacher costumed in yet another existence, a more peaceful one set in "those days . . . until the war came. . . . 'Oh no,' " he hesitates, " 'I forget, you're young, you've never known it.' "[84]

Without its connecting realities, this, like many other scenes, becomes a disruption in the otherwise fast-moving spy film. The problem is caused not by the transformation of monologue into dialogue but by the removal of the contemplative level of the story in the process. The result is that lines that are very important in the novel become truisms masquerading as profundities in the film. So Beatrice's response to Wormold's confession pales. "We should be loyal to love not to countries," she quips, as she fades off the screen to make room for the extremely funny checkers sequence. And Hasselbacher's "As long as you invent you do no harm" is hackneyed as it gives way to Wormold at the country club.

Without the parallel between Wormold and the novelist, the lines not only disrupt the flow of the film, but show Wormold to be more knowledgeable about life in general than his naïveté in the movie warrants. Sometimes he even seems out of character, as when he is forced to kill Carter. His hesitation should reinforce his humility, his love for the individual, and his ability to laugh at himself—all the qualities that endear him to us. But it does not. The cinematic Wormold loses stature in this scene and becomes farcical as he recognizes human idiosyncrasies.

Guinness says that he and Reed had a difference of opinion about how Wormold should be played. Reed felt that "the character is a plain man. It is important that he should not stand out." Guinness, on the other hand, believed he "should have been playing Wormold as a much more clearly defined character, an untidy, defeated sort of man, the kind of person you would see in London with the *New Statesman and Nation* sticking out of his back pocket."[85] Reed was right, of course. Wormold *is* a plain man, and Guinness plays him as Greene wrote him. He is the innocent who is moved along by forces that become real around him. Guinness's sweet smile, his completely credulous face, which so often appears in close-up, his easy relief when danger has passed, these and the many other features that keep him somewhat separate from the action are quite appropriate. Wormold should stay the same, even if frightened and saddened by what has happened. It is the atmosphere around him that should shift.

Reed tried to accomplish this by changing the lighting so that at the beginning of the film the atmosphere was set for comedy. "That is," Reed explained, "rather brightly and flatly. . . . Then as the picture moves toward melodrama, we . . . shoot with a wide angle lens getting the effect of the walls closing in. We . . . use sharp hard lights in the night exteriors, making the street slick and shiny, getting a brittle black-and-white feeling."[86] But although effective, Reed's lighting is not enough to carry Wormold through the heavier scenes.

Greene believes that the problem lies with Jo Morrow, who played Milly and gave Guinness no leeway. "All the scenes she was in were bad," he says, "except the cemetery sequence. That was well done. She just couldn't act. Reed should have listened to Noel Coward who told him so when he first met her."[87] She was too old for the part and played a far too dishonest and seductive Milly, missing the spoiled adolescent entirely. She made Wormold's naïve desire to give his daughter everything and eventually send her to a school in Switzerland look silly. But if her tartish behavior with Segura made Wormold's dreams for her appear rather stupid instead of misguided as in the book, it had little to do with the lack of integration of the contemplative side of Wormold's character into the spy spoof.

There is another problem as well. This is a story about how individuals are used by governments in a game of cold war. The world is a large checkerboard played on by the global powers; ordinary people are the pieces; anyone is used; any place is vulnerable. One side accelerates its moves in counteraction to what bumblers like Wormold and the men in London do. The innocent fall; the bumblers survive and are sometimes even rewarded.

But someone commits the violence. In the story one of those people is Captain Segura. War used to be uniforms and gentlemen, Hasselbacher tells us; now it is spies and secrecy and tortures. Yet Segura is let off by Greene. He is not very different from anyone else in the film except that he has a cigarette case made of human skin and drives a convertible surrounded by a motorcade of his police. He frequents Milly's club; he chats with the nuns at her convent school; he brings her home to an unruffled father. He even appears mildly funny in the checkers scene and somewhat charming as he sends Wormold off to safety and an OBE. This is light treatment indeed against a background of violent death and people identified as torturable or untorturable. The far less sadistic Harry Lime received a much harsher sentence.

Here again, however, the uneven treatment of Segura and Batista's Cuba cannot be resolved without the novel's allusion to Wormold as author. His position of innocence must be seen as a simple fidelity to his own vision. When the episodes of violence build up and the other characters' lives are changed, Wormold's refusal to learn from experience must be seen, as it is in the book, to reveal his particular sense of morality and responsibility. We, after all, do see the violence if he does not, and we are not as quick to overlook Segura's sinister role in Cuba as he is. As an innocent author, Wormold may pass through Havana untouched, but without him in this role the novel's satire is largely lost. We are left with a somewhat too dashing captain and a rather too silly vacuum-cleaner salesman, which is hardly what Greene intended.

Yet although the film lacked the bitter irony of the original and was thus aesthetically flawed from the critics' point of view, it was not unsuccessful at the box office. The Greene-Reed team could still draw crowds, even in America, where the movie broke box-office records when it opened in New York, and even among the smaller, more sophisticated audiences of the late 1950s. Yet it was obviously not the success the earlier Greene-Reed films had been. With dis-

appointment and apology critics concluded that it was a more difficult movie to make than *The Fallen Idol* or *The Third Man.*

It was certainly an unfortunate finish to a decade of cinematic work
that Greene had begun with such anticipation. The promise of
filming with Reed did not bring its expected reward, and by the time
Our Man in Havana was made, the British film industry had fallen on
such bad times that even the studio of Greene's old and successful
friend Alexander Korda had been forced to shut. Cinema attendance,
which had reached a peak of 31 million a week in 1946, had dropped
to 9.9 million by 1960. British Lion was only one of many studios to
close. Others, like Ealing, were sold to television, and directors and
actors who in the postwar years had made "those unique essays on
British character and manners that gave films from Britian their
special distinction and appeal"[88] either moved to Hollywood or
turned their attention to jointly financed movies made for the international market.

Greene's and Reed's successes of 1948 and 1949 belonged to a
different period in film history, "a popular cinema which was never
likely to come again."[89] And, in a sense, so did Greene's canon of the
common and the poetic. His belief that movies should be popular and
realistic arose just when the mass media began to assume their full
importance and when, simultaneously, there was great concern that
ordinary people were being made passive by the commercialization of
leisure. *The Fallen Idol, The Third Man* and, indeed, *Brighton Rock*
were successful because they achieved a high degree of artistic distinction and also because they were exactly what the cinema was calling
for, realism plus relaxing entertainment. But *Our Man in Havana*, a
film very much about British character and manners, was made for a
cinema no longer inhabited by those vast audiences who demanded
the unpretentious and easygoing films that Greene's formula had
counted on. The new viewer wanted something "introspective, . . .
sensitive to intellectual and social questions, sexually mature, with
refreshing and un-Americanized insights into other cultures, other
values, and other peoples. . . . Movies had . . . become an elitist, not a
popular art."[90]

Our Man in Havana might easily have fulfilled these new criteria,
but its more serious side did not survive Greene's adaptation. Yet it
was not a film for the masses either. Although lightened in that
direction, it moved perhaps too fast intellectually and left the viewer

wondering why Wormold was so naïve. One might speculate that, like J. Arthur Rank, who lost over $8 million in the early 1950s trying to sell extravaganzas to America when he might have made money at home with smaller ventures in the manner of *The Winslow Boy, Mine Own Executioner, The Fallen Idol*, or *The Small Back Room*, Greene and Reed had misjudged the nature of their audience in 1959. But to look at *Our Man in Havana* as a film that did not quite make the transition from the style of the forties to that of the late fifties is to overlook the film's serious aesthetic problems. It is better to regard it as a failed attempt to handle Greene's writing of that period, which had become more introspective and philosophical than his earlier work, and far more difficult to adapt.

When Greene wrote his next script, for *The Comedians*, he was able to keep the political and philosophical ideas of the novel intact by breaking long passages of dialogue with sequences of intense action. As well as producing deep irony, the juxtapositions allowed his characters to discuss ideas in a fairly methodical, sometimes even theatrical, way. Adapting *Our Man in Havana* may simply have uprooted his penchant for lightening his work for the films, as it did his belief that he and Reed could inevitably produce magic on the screen. Its failure certainly caused him to turn his back on the cinema for several years, and when he returned, it was no longer to attempt popular movies.

In January, 1959, he went to the Belgian Congo with *A Burnt-Out Case* beginning to form in his head. The book was to be his blackest, and in it he would discover Comedy.

Alexander Korda and Graham Greene on Korda's yacht, the Elsewhere, during the 1950s. Courtesy of Michael Korda.

Noel Coward as Hawthorne, Alec Guinness as Wormold, and Burl Ives as Dr. Hasselbacher in *Our Man in Havana,* 1959. Courtesy of The Museum of Modern Art, Film Stills Archive.

Jo Morrow as Milly, Alec Guinness as Wormold, and Ernie Kovacs as Segura in *Our Man in Havana*, 1959. Courtesy of The Museum of Modern Art, Film Stills Archive.

5

The Written Word

A novelist who knows the business of film making to be hostile to his talents should not be surprised by a decade of poor adaptations of his work. It is true that before the 1950s Greene had won great acclaim for his movies, had been heralded as a cinematic writer, and had himself regarded the film medium with very high hopes. But he had also been forced to make endless aesthetic concessions to the financeers of the business, had known that verbal and visual images have their own identities, and had more often than not been disappointed by the films that bore his name.

Yet in 1958 he was bitter enough at his bad luck to attack everyone involved in the film making process:

> . . . actors, directors and cameramen who are paid, and paid handsomely, whatever the result. They can always put the blame for a disaster elsewhere which no novelist can. . . . We have to learn our craft more painfully, more meticulously. . . . As a writer one hasn't the blind optimism of the film-maker who believes against all evidence that

somehow the wrong actors, the wrong director, the wrong cameraman, the wrong art-director, the wrong colour-process, will all come together and produce a lucky accident.[1]

His attack was not ill-founded. The fifties' adaptations were riddled with cinematic error and transgressed widely from his original intention. To make matters worse, the production of his first plays, *The Living Room* (1953) and *The Potting Shed* (1957), had given him such immediate pleasure that his experience with film making soured in contrast. Yet perhaps Greene's condemnation of the film making process was not entirely fair. During the forties and early fifties his writing had changed in ways that must have made some of his novels even more difficult to adapt than the earlier books had been. And in 1958 he had not approached, except subjectively, the large question of what he should expect when he saw his work on the screen.

During and just after the war he had written that small cluster of novels that gained him what he now calls the "detestable"[2] title "Catholic writer." The group was foreshadowed by *Brighton Rock* in 1938 and included *The Power and the Glory* (1940), *The Heart of the Matter* (1948) and *The End of the Affair* (1951). *A Burnt-Out Case* (1961) might be added to the list, but since it is about the loss of faith, and is that novel in which Comedy was discovered, it is better placed with the later comicopolitical books.

Written during the same period were other novels that were not religiously oriented. These are *The Confidential Agent* (1939) and *The Ministry of Fear* (1943), which have more in common with the earlier social books, and *Loser Takes All* (1955), *The Quiet American* (1955), and *Our Man in Havana* (1958), which are more like the later political books. There were also plays, some of which had religious themes, and stories and films, including *The Third Man*, most of which did not.

Clearly, in half of what he wrote during this period, Greene was wrestling with religious concerns different from those that dominated his work before the war. The seminal preoccupation in the early fiction had been the relationship between the self, society and the historical process; in the Catholic novels it is primarily between the self and God. What is not obvious is that with this thematic change came a rebalancing in the nexus of empirical and psychological reality at the heart of his prose that had previously made his novels so appealing to film makers.

In the 1930s, Greene had paid increasing attention to his characters' social positions and had used appropriate detail to explain their psychological problems and hence their actions. The characters were engaged in a social war. It was far from the Marxist notion of a class war, for his capitalists were only a small segment of their class, and his poor were not in the technical sense proletarian; they existed in the social penumbra between the petite bourgeoisie and the organized working class. Nevertheless, Greene was concerned to identify as society's victims those individuals, especially the poor, who could not exercise any control over their own lives, and to root their problems in easily identifiable social detail. Although his protagonists were often society's deviants, they were common people like those who, by and large, filled the cinemas of that decade.

One of the ways he drew our attention to the importance of his characters' social situations was by making marks of their class constantly visible. The position of the director of Conrad Drover's firm in *It's a Battlefield*, for example, was indicated by his "light suit and . . . public-school tie."[3] The Assistant Commissioner in the same novel had "thin lips and . . . . upper class lids."[4] Raven's harelip in *A Gun for Sale* "was like a badge of class. It revealed the poverty of parents who couldn't afford a clever surgeon."[5] These details were visible links between the conflict raging on the social battlefield of prewar Britain and the psychological torments of the characters. They explained behavior: in *England Made Me*, Krogh was "hopelessly conditioned"[6] by his wealth; in *Stamboul Train*, Coral's tactics with Myatt arose from her "accumulated experience of poverty."[7] And they formed an easily recognizable base from which Greene spun ambience. In other words, they contributed to that bond of common reality which Greene felt a writer should share with his reader. Behavior was far from simple, but expressed this way it could nevertheless be quickly understood by readers and, more important for our purposes, by the cinema's large, undiscriminating audience.

When Greene was film critic, he tightened the bond between empirical and psychological reality in his own writing and learned to cut and juxtapose scenes in a cinematic way to lend his work great visual precision. Between 1935 and 1940 the relationships among the characters also changed. In the early thirties brutality in the novels was isolated, but as Europe darkened, corruption and violence pervaded the entire social structure of the books, and class war in England was assimilated to the war that loomed on the Continent. As the scene widened, Greene juxtaposed the delinquency of small criminals with the villainy of industrial magnates in such a way that the misdemeanors of the proletariat of crime, the Ravens and Pinkies who got their hands dirty, diminished into venialness. When this happened, the characters lost all belief in man's ability to stop the rising brutality and social rot, they trusted each other less, and they retreated into their own private worlds. In *Stamboul Train*, for example, though Czinner was bungling and ineffective, he was a public man armed with a plan for the future of mankind. By *England Made Me*, Tony says he is "not young enough to believe in a juster world, not old enough for the country, the king, the trenches to mean anything . . . at all."[8] In *Brighton Rock* the world has become hell, and man is forced to struggle alone to survive. By *The Ministry of Fear*, Rowe's inability to live in the world, which has become "a madhouse,"[9] causes his complete psychological withdrawal.

As the characters retreated from each other into their own psychological dilemmas, Greene allegorically heightened empirical reality so that by *The Confidential Agent* and *The Ministry of Fear* it had come to reflect the mind of the protagonist almost completely. The tightness of the imagery in these late social novels made them difficult to film, and the adaptations of these books missed much of their protagonists' psychological complexities.

The Ministry of Fear synthesizes the concerns of the early social period of Greene's writing while making a transition to the more private spiritual preoccupations that characterize his religious novels. From the beginning of that book, which is set in and around London during World War II, a good deal of time is spent in the England of Rowe's schooldays: "The fête called him like innocence: it was entangled in childhood, with vicarage gardens, and girls in white summer frocks, and the smell of herbaceous borders, and security."[10] One can recognize several autobiographical details in the novel, Rowe's excursion through the green baize door, for example, to the nightmare world of Dr. Forester, who is initially a father figure to him. But what is important is that Rowe remembers the same middle-class Edwardian world that Greene grew up in. Here is the security of patterns, of a culture intact, where the ruling class is believed to have the social good at heart, and where everyone else is thought to be comfortable.

In contrast is the childhood world remade into a madhouse resembling the settings of thrillers:

Tea on the lawn, evensong, croquet, the old ladies calling, the gentle unmalicious gossip, the gardener trundling the wheelbarrow full of leaves and grass. People write about it as if it still went on; . . . but it's not there any more. . . . You remember St. Clement's—the bells of St. Clement's? They've smashed that—St. James's Piccadilly, the Burlington Arcade, Garland's Hotel where we stayed for the pantomime, Maples, and John Lewis. It sounds like a thriller, doesn't it?—but the thrillers are like life. . . . You used to laugh at the books Miss Savage read—about spies, and murders and violence, and wild motor-car chases, but, dear, that's real life: it's what we've all made of the world since you died. . . . The world has been remade.[11]

Caught in a nightmare of brutality, fear, alienation, and helplessness, man can neither escape nor stop the process of change that he witnesses. The remade world is now home; "there isn't anywhere else at all."[12] So the social nightmare is internalized and becomes the psychological analogue of Rowe's moral dilemma. In the childhood Edwardian world "God is good, the grown-up man or woman knows the answer to every question, there is such a thing as truth, and justice is as measured and faultless as a clock."[13] But in the adult, remade world, things are immeasurably more complicated. If Rowe has killed his wife to end her pain and his fear of having to watch it, then it follows that everything has more than one side. "It wasn't only evil men who did these things. Courage smashes a cathedral, endurance lets a city starve, pity kills . . . we are trapped and betrayed by our virtues."[14]

Ostensibly, Rowe's problem is his inability to adjust to the burden of guilt he bears from having killed his wife. Substantially, his nightmare is broader and encompasses the moral dilemma of the liberal. Rowe is the good man caught up as he tries to see every side of all issues and behave decently in a world where the old values are smashed and most of the new ones are unacceptable. In losing his memory, he reverts to a childlike state in which he temporarily escapes not only the nightmare of ambiguity that the remade world forces on him but the necessity to make choices. In other words, amnesia offers him temporary moral and political immobility.

Here, when Greene's work expresses such despair about man's lack of collective well-being, Catholicism enters the novels. It is not inserted intellectually. Nor is it used as a solution to the madhouse Europe has become. It arises as a frightened and arrogant threat from Pinkie and Rose, who believe they have some inside information about the real workings of things. "There's things *you* don't know" Rose tells Ida. But she and Pinkie do. "They were two Romans together in the grey street. They understood each other."[15] And the kernel of this secret knowledge is that as Raven's crimes in *A Gun for Sale* were insignificant when compared with Sir Marcus's, so right and wrong in the social, historical sense, have no meaning because "their taste was extinguished by stronger foods—Good and Evil."[16]

In 1933, Greene wrote that Henry James's novels "are only saved from the deepest cynicism by the religious sense; the struggle between the beautiful and the treacherous is lent, as in Hardy's novels, the importance of the supernatural, human nature is not despicable . . . for . . . [it is] capable of damnation."[17] One might say the same of the introduction of Catholicism into Greene's books: that with it he attempts to save them from his own cynicism and despair at "the moment when civilisation really begins to lose grip, when violence becomes an end in itself,"[18] and when men isolate themselves to survive.

But if the introduction of Catholicism saved the novels in this way, it also made them more difficult to film, for they continued to withdraw further from that base of recognizable reality out of which the earlier books sprang. When Greene's characters looked to Catholicism for a new direction, having concluded that the social formations of their world were inimical to them, his prose drew away from filmable material reality into the more personal world of the mind. This is not to say that 1930s themes were not carried over. The plots still followed patterns of pursuit, and the protagonists were still marginal. Like Pinkie, who never questioned the structure of his society but persisted in acting against its rules, the Catholic characters maintained faith in the church's teachings while behaving contrary to the tenets of its doctrine.

What was different about the characters was that, unlike Pinkie or Raven, who actively sought solutions, however misguided, to their social predicaments, the protagonists of the religious novels gave in to the inevitability of their situations in a world where suffering, death, and alienation were more pervasive than they were in the earlier books. They endured their lot in a private arena where Catholic knowledge provided an exclusive, if tormenting, explanation for their existence. And human relations were seen as compromising in these books. Although Scobie and the whisky priest gained stature because they acted in humanitarian ways, one always felt their acts were less important than their religious commitments. Perhaps that was because they had lost faith not only in man's goodness but also in his future.

When this happened, the novels moved away from the daily concerns of the masses and from that juxtaposition between what is and what might be, which, as film critic Greene claimed made good cinema. External events shrank in importance and were abstracted. It was as though when the characters retreated into their own spiritual concerns Greene's prose turned inward on itself, retreating from material reality to a position where as literature it ordered the world. The writing still appeared to be as cinematic as ever. It had the same Dickensian plasticity about it in its extraordinarily optical quality, the same Eisensteinian rigor in its achievement of continuity through montage, and the same Griersonian tension in its insistence on distilling character from ordinary things. But the balance between empirical and psychological reality was shifted in ways that bound its images even more stubbornly to paper.

In *Brighton Rock* and the social novels before it, material existence was the base for psychological and spiritual exploration. Psychological torments, and in Pinkie religious hopes, were couched in documentary realism. The internal was always firmly bound to the external because society was seen to be the cause of the protagonists' dilemmas.

In the Catholic novels, on the contrary, it is the internal religious obsession of the protagonist that conditions the plot. The geography of the whisky priest's voyage, for example, appears to have the same cinematic possibility as Pinkie's Brighton, but in fact it does not. Material reality has dissolved into various aspects that have become more or less disconnected from each other; in the whisky priest we have a religious explanation of things, in the lieutenant, a thin political interpretation. In *The End of the Affair* Sarah's is a religious view, Bendrix's a social one. This is not the same as Greene's earlier tendency to stereotype characters so that Pinkie and Rose, for example, appeared as opposite sides of the same coin, or Crane and Chase in *Rumour at Nightfall* as the heart and mind separated. In the religious novels we have interpretations of reality, not human characteristics, in opposition. The result is that the religious protagonists are cut off, except peripherally, from cinematic material. Although they move through vividly wrought topographies, their lives are largely concerned with the intellectual experiences of heaven and hell. Pinkie's aspirations were irrevocably connected to the tangible injustices of Brighton, but the whisky priest has neither belief nor interest in material reality. He breathes and suffers in Mexico, but he lives in his religious imagination. Brighton was the cause of Pinkie's being; Mexico is a projection of the whisky priest's and is consequently less accessible to the camera.

As an extended example, take the mass he says for the people of Brigitta's village. Like most of Greene's other scenes this one appears potentially cinematic. The set is enclosed in a hut. "Perhaps two dozen people sat on the earth floor . . . while he preached to them." Even the focus and angle of vision are defined:

> He couldn't see them with any distinctness. The candles on the packing-case smoked steadily upwards—the door was shut and there was no current of air. He was talking about heaven, standing between them and the candles in the ragged peon trousers and the torn shirt. They grunted and moved restlessly. He knew they were longing for the Mass to be over: they had woken him very early, because there were rumours of police.[19]

A cameraman might easily take over here. The lens focusing, the costuming, the lighting, even the direction the plot will take are all built into the passage. But as the mass begins, the writing becomes less and less concrete. The dialogue is interspersed with what the whisky priest thinks, with flashbacks to his past and intimations of his future. By the end of the scene we see that the emphasis is on his interior monologue. The celebration of the mass has been visually routine, its importance disconnected from empirical reality:

> "The police are on the way. They are only a mile off, coming through the forest."
>
> This was what he was used to: the words not striking home, the hurried close, the expectation of pain coming between him and his faith. He said stubbornly, "Above all remember this—heaven is here." Were they on horseback or on foot? If they were on foot, he had twenty minutes left to finish Mass and hide. "Here now, at this minute, your fear and my fear are part of heaven, where there will be no fear any more for ever." He turned his back on them and began very quickly to recite the Credo. There was a time when he had approached the Canon of the Mass with actual physical dread—the first time he had consumed the body of God in a state of mortal sin. But then life bred its excuses—it hadn't after a

while seemed to matter very much, whether he was damned or not, so long as these others . . . .

He kissed the top of the packing-case and turned to bless. In the inadequate light he could just see two men kneeling with their arms stretched out in the shape of a cross—they would keep that position until the consecration was over, one more mortification squeezed out of their harsh and painful lives. He felt humbled by the pain ordinary men bore voluntarily; his pain was forced on him. "Oh Lord, I have loved the beauty of thy house . . ." The candles smoked and the people shifted on their knees—an absurd happiness bobbed up in him again before anxiety returned: it was as if he had been permitted to look in from the outside at the population of heaven. Heaven must contain just such sacred and dutiful and hunger-lined faces. For a matter of seconds he felt an immense satisfaction that he could talk of suffering to them now without hypocrisy—it is hard for the sleek and well-fed priest to praise poverty. He began the praise for the living: the long list of the Apostles and Martyrs fell like footsteps—Cornelii, Cypriani, Laurentii, Chrysogoni—soon the police would reach the clearing where his mule had sat down under him and he had washed in the pool. The Latin words ran into each other on his hasty tongue: he could feel impatience all round him. He began the Consecration of the Host (he had finished the wafers long ago—it was a piece of bread from Maria's oven); impatience abruptly died away: everything in time became a routine but this—"Who the day before he suffered took Bread into his holy and venerable hands . . ." Whoever moved outside on the forest path, there was no movement here—"*Hoc est enim Corpus Meum.*" He could hear the sigh of breaths released: God was here in the body for the first time in six years. When he raised the Host he could imagine the faces lifted like famished dogs. He began the Consecration of the Wine—in a chipped cup. That was one more surrender—for two years he had carried a chalice round with him; once it would have cost him his life, if the police officer who opened his case had not been a Catholic. It may very well have cost the officer his life, if anybody had discovered the evasion—he didn't know; you went round making God knew what martyrs—in Concepción or elsewhere—when you yourself were without grace enough to die.

The Consecration was in silence: no bell rang. He knelt by the packing-case exhausted, without a prayer. Somebody opened the door; a voice whispered urgently, "They're here."[20]

The setting is of vital consequence here, but the action is not in any way visible. Without the interior monologue the whole scene would fall flat; indeed, it would be without any significance at all. Although the sequence takes its direction from material reality in that the mass becomes real to the priest only as he compares the peons' suffering with his own, the drama is entirely internal. All we "see" in the scene is the restlessness of people awaiting the inevitable arrival of the police.

Action is similarly often invisible in *The Heart of the Matter*. At the beginning of Book 3, part 2, Scobie and Helen sit in the car outside Helen's house. She tells him that she is going to leave and with her departure he will be all right. " 'You'll see. You'll be able to clean up. You'll be a Catholic again.' . . . 'I want to stop giving pain,' " Scobie replies. As the dialogue continues, his untold desire to die is spliced into it so that the spoken words diminish in importance until they finally serve only to ricochet Scobie's thoughts: " 'Don't speak, dear. I'm really being quite good,' " Helen says. "He thought again: if I were dead, she would be free of me: one forgets the dead quickly; one doesn't wonder about the dead—what is he doing now, who is he with? This for her is the hard way. 'Now, dear,' " she goes on. " 'I'm going to do it. Shut your eyes. Count three showly, and I won't be in sight.' . . . Oh God," Scobie prays, "his hands dripping over the wheel, kill me now. My God, you'll never have more complete contrition. What a mess I am. I carry suffering with me like a body smell. Kill me. Put an end to me. Vermin don't have to exterminate themselves. Kill me. Now. Now. . . . 'Shut your eyes, dear. This is the end. Really the end.' She said hopelessly."[21]

This direction continues through the next several scenes with Louise's conversation spurring on Scobie's death wish, and then Dr. Travis's tentative diagnosis of angina offering him a practical solution. After the examination we find him sitting in his car with his package of medicine on the seat beside him. "I have only now to choose the date," he thinks, as he drives down toward the police station and stops at the church. There what began as a dialogue with Helen and became a partial interior monologue with Louise and Dr. Travis ends a complete internalization. But "no one can speak a monologue for long alone," we are told, as Greene interjects "another voice [that] will always make itself heard: every monologue sooner or later becomes a discussion. So now he couldn't keep the other voice silent: it spoke from the cave of his body."[22]

In juxtaposing dialogue and interior monologue, Greene changes the point of view back and forth between the characters and eventual-

ly adds his own voice. It is an effective and unobtrusive method of
shifting the focal point and is very close to the way dialogue is
presented on film when we watch the face of one character and
simultaneously listen to the voice of another. But Scobie's and
Helen's entire conversation would be impossible to transfer to the
screen because it extends far beyond what is said into something like
the introspection we saw in *The Name of Action* and *The Man Within*.
As in the whisky priest's mass, visible realism rapidly gives way to
the workings of the individual mind. Very little is public. Scobie
passively performs one series of acts while concentrating on quite
another so that the real action occurs far away from the camera's eye.

   In the earlier social novels the visible had stood alone without
intellectual interpretation. Now it has become almost inseparable
from the characters' deliberations. If we compare the sequence in *A
Gun for Sale* where Raven considers his reflection in a barber's window
and another in *The Power and the Glory* in which the whisky priest sees
his photo in the lieutenant's office, we can see the tightened link
between empirical detail and thought:

> Raven had been on his feet all morning. He had to keep moving; he
> couldn't use the little change he had on food, because he did not dare to
> stay still, to give anyone the chance to study his face. He bought a paper
> outside the post office and saw his own description there, printed in black
> type inside a frame. He was angry because it was on a back page: the
> situation in Europe filled the first page. By midday, moving here and
> moving there with his eyes always open for Cholmondeley, he was
> dog-tired. He stood for a moment and stared at his own face in a barber's
> window; ever since his flight from the café he had remained unshaven; a
> moustache would hide his scar, but he knew from experience how his hair
> grew in patches, strong on the chin, weak on the lip, and not at all on
> either side of the red deformity. Now the scrubby growth on his chin was
> making him conspicuous and he didn't dare go into the barber's for a
> shave.[23]

The prose is flat and direct. Raven is observed from the outside as a
camera might film him looking at himself.

   In contrast, Greene's description of the whisky priest's picture is
multifaceted and complex before he gets to see it:

> A large number of people sat round a table: young girls in white muslin:
> older women with untidy hair and harassed expressions: a few men peered
> shyly and solicitously out of the background. All the faces were made up

of small dots. It was a newspaper photograph of a first communion party taken years ago; a youngish man in a Roman collar sat among the women. You could imagine him petted with small delicacies, preserved for their use in the stifling atmosphere of intimacy and respect. He sat there, plump, with protuberant eyes, bubbling with harmless feminine jokes.[24]

The description is slanted. The women are harassed, the men few, shy, and solicitous. At this point in the narrative the photograph is used to tell us as much about the lieutenant as about the priest. Later, when the lieutenant returns to his office, the photograph again implements characterization:

On the wall of the office the gangster still stared stubbornly in profile towards the first communion party. Somebody had inked round the priest's head to detach him from the girls' and the womens' faces: the unbearable grin peeked out of a halo. The lieutenant called furiously out onto the patio, "Is there nobody here?"[25]

And finally the priest himself sees it:

He named a random village: he was absorbed in his own portrait. There he sat among the white-starched dresses of the first communicants. Somebody had put a ring round his face to pick it out. There was another picture on the wall too—the gringo from San Antonio, Texas, wanted for murder and bank robbery.[26]

The photograph has told us little of the whisky priest. It does not exist in its own right as Raven's reflection in the barber's window does. It is entangled with the lieutenant's character and because of its juxtaposition with the gringo's portrait is used to foreshadow the future.

But the whisky priest's photograph is only an isolated example. Throughout the novel seemingly empirical detail is no longer what it appears. It has been allegorically heightened to create a density of atmosphere perhaps unequaled in Greene's writing but far too abstract for the camera to catch with much success.

In the opening pages of *The Power and the Glory*, for instance, one finds the same attention to detail that allowed Boulting to film Brighton exactly as Greene had written of it. We have a cinematographer's view of Mr. Tench as he crosses the square. There are vultures flapping over the town: "over the tiny plaza, over the bust of an ex-president, ex-general, ex-human being, over the two stalls which sold mineral water, towards the river and the sea." A man with a gun sits "in a small patch of shade against a wall." The river runs "heavily by towards the sea between the banana plantations." The *General Obregon* is "tied up to the bank, and beer was being unloaded—a hundred cases were already stacked upon the quay." Even the details of the boat are given. She is "about thirty yards long. A few feet of damaged rail, one life boat, a bell hanging on a rotten cord, an oil lamp in the bow."[27]

This is the kind of documentary realism that Greene perfected in the novels he wrote while he was a film critic. The details of setting are combined as though everything real were visible, and the whole description moves as in a long panning shot. Yet juxtaposed with the flat accumulation of detail is the beginning of a process by which the empirical is abstracted. The vultures "looked down from the roof with shabby indifference." In the novel's second line the visible is already qualified and used to begin the process of characterization. Mr. Tench "wasn't carrion yet. A faint feeling of rebellion stirred in . . . [his] heart, and he wrenched up a piece of the road with splintering finger-nails and tossed it feebly towards them. One rose," and we are off with it over the town to the river. But it "wouldn't find anything there: the sharks looked after the carrion on that side."

This is no straightforward record of the plaza. It is heavily slanted with the smell of imprisonment and death. Nothing human exists here. Even the bust of the former president is metamorphosed into a former human being. Very rapidly the present is projected onto an image of the future in which Mr. Tench will become carrion, and from there almost simultaneously we are thrust back to his past. The man with the gun draws the comment: " . . . it wasn't like England; the man said nothing at all, just stared malevolently up at Mr. Tench, as if he had never had any dealings with the foreigner." As we pass the Treasury, "which had once been a church," the present and past are again joined. We see the building, but its new purpose spells a political change. And then history gives way to the sun and dust. "Mr. Tench went sweating by. . . . he suddenly forgot what he had come out for."[28]

Time is compressed. As in film, the past, present, and future mingle without heeding chronological order so that everything seems to exist simultaneously. On first reading, in fact, time seems unimportant because characterization and tone have been shaped from

spatial detail, and as the story progresses, it appears almost nonexis-
tent. It is the priest's journey, not its duration, that occupies us, with
its emphasis on the weight of the hot, humid air, the dust, the sheer
physical difficulty of the situation. How many days the voyage takes
is unimportant in comparison, and we do not hurry toward the end
because we know it will bring only death. Our preoccupation with
how the whisky priest passes through the topography of the novel
appears cinematic, of course, for it is through the penetration and
delineation of space that the camera creates meaning. But if we look
at the opening sequences of the book again, we see that, although we
have concentrated on the setting, time is nevertheless vital. Even in
the flat acknowledgment of the bust on the plaza, an image that
moves exactly as Eisenstein's sleeping, sitting, crouching lion in
Battleship Potemkin, it is the passage of time that tells the tale. History
has determined the statue's new definition as it has also changed the
church into the Treasury.

When a few paragraphs later we come to Mr. Tench's meeting
with the customs man, again time seems cinematically suspended,
but it is in fact intricately woven into the fabric of the atmosphere:

> "The set is nearly finished. Tonight," he promised wildly. It was, of
> course, quite impossible; but that was how one lived, putting off
> everything. The man was satisfied: he might forget, and in any case what
> could he *do*? He had paid in advance. That was the whole world to Mr.
> Tench: the heat and the forgetting, the putting off till tomorrow, if
> possible cash down—for what? He stared out over the slow river: the fin
> of a shark moved like a periscope at the river's mouth. In the course of
> years several ships had stranded and they now helped to prop up the
> bank, the smoke-stacks leaning over like guns pointing at some distant
> objective across the banana trees and the swamps.
>   Mr. Tench thought: ether cylinder: I nearly forgot.[29]

Here, as so often in Greene's novels, we have prose that has a
cinematic quality but is almost unadaptable. Even when its images
are strikingly visual, the demands of the similes confine them stubbornly to paper: "the shadow of the custom's house," we are told,
"shifted a few inches farther toward the river: the vulture moved a
little, like the black hand of a clock."

As in film, order is derived from the shaping of empirical reality,
and tenses converge to lend the sense of simultaneity. Mr. Tench's
past is almost inseparable from the present:

Home lay like a picture post card on a pile of other postcards: shuffle the pack and you had Nottingham, a Metroland birth-place, an interlude in Southend. Mr. Tench's father had been a dentist too—his first memory was finding a discarded cast in a wastepaper basket—the rough toothless gaping mouth of clay, like something dug up in Dorset—Neanderthal or Pithecanthropus. It had been his favourite toy: they tried to tempt him with Meccano, but fate had struck. There is always one moment in childhood when the door opens and lets the future in.[30]

Yet the continuity of exterior reality has disintegrated: Mr. Tench cannot remember from one paragraph to another why he has come into the plaza, and the buildings and statues he passes are not what they appear. An order has been imposed on material matter that has little to do with what a camera might record and everything to do with Mr. Tench's interpretation. Things have been allegorically changed so that the incidents and objects as we might see them are saturated with his notions about them, which come from the past as much as the present and include projections into the future. And as so often with Greene's metaphors, the usual order of allegorical presentation, in which abstractions are made concrete, is reversed. Mr. Tench's frame of mind is squeezed from the detail of the setting; the setting is not used to make it more tangible. Concrete detail has produced a complex and abstract reality held together by Mr. Tench's mind and obstinately confined to print.

Interestingly, this unfilmable internalization does not occur in *The Third Man*, which was written toward the end of the religious period, or in *The End of the Affair*. No doubt *The Third Man*'s subject and the fact that it was intended for the cinema in the first place account for its stylistic difference. *The End of the Affair* is another matter. Of the three Catholic novels it is the only one written in the first person. In it thoughts are externalized through the use of diaries, letters, and narrator's comments. Although a diary would appear a private rendering sometimes used, as by Scobie, to conceal intentions and hide action, Sarah's journal is a public document used to dramatize her feelings. We look over Bendrix's shoulder as he reads her secret thoughts and juxtapose her story with his. In this way she is watched from inside and outside the narrative, and her actions are interpreted by herself, by Bendrix, and by us.

This modulating first-person point of view acts something like the cataloguing of detail in the earlier novels. We have accumulated views of the same action here, as Sarah's and Bendrix's individual accounts of their lunch at Rules. The method allows distance between the experiencing and the recording of an event so that thought is externalized and prevented from becoming the one-sided monologue it is in *The Power and the Glory* and *The Heart of the Matter*. Feelings are presented intimately, but they stand on their own to be examined from different angles and ordered in such a way that they might be turned into cinematic action.

Sometimes Greene makes this transition from thought to dramatic activity within the novel itself, as when Bendrix whispers to Sarah while she sleeps:

> Suddenly I realised she was asleep. . . .
>
> Children are supposed to be influenced by what you whisper to them in their sleep, and I began to whisper to Sarah, not loud enough to wake her. . . . "I love you, Sarah," I whispered. "Nobody has ever loved you as much before. We are going to be happy. Henry won't mind. . . . He'll find himself a new habit to take your place. . . . We are going away. . . . Nobody can stop it now. You love me, Sarah."[31]

In Greene's first play, *The Living Room*, which was written just after *The End of the Affair*, we find him obliged to rely reavily on the spoken word for effect as he does here, using techniques he successfully employed in the movies. In *The End of the Affair* he turns feelings into dialogue and disconnects them from ambience, allowing the spoken word to carry its full weight in a way he had not since the novels he wrote when he was a film critic.

This modulating first-person point of view in *The End of the Affair* also allows him to place his own comments in the text unobtrusively. When Bendrix tells us Sarah is asleep, Greene interjects into the dialogue his own maxim: "Children are supposed to be influenced by what you whisper to them in their sleep." We take the statement as coming from Greene's novelist-narrator, but in fact it comes from his own omniscient pen. He uses Bendrix, as he used Calloway in *The Third Man*, in the manner a cinematographer uses his camera. It is Bendrix who records the story but Greene who comments on it by shifting the focus of our attention from him and by selecting information to create irony. In this way the novel becomes a study of itself; it records a process of action through which the narrator makes sense of what has happened to him. He begins by claiming to be an uncommitted recorder of past events, but as Greene selects what he sees, we soon discover that Bendrix's very presence as narrator involves him in the action. As he relives the past by recording it, we watch him discover his role in it.

Of course, Greene has always inserted his own comments into his novels as he does in *The End of the Affair*. In the earliest books the intrusion was open and obvious. After Chase in *Rumour at Nightfall* has appealed to Eulelia to love him, Greene comments:

> The appeal . . . was not made in vain. The expression of rectitude itself was a partial agreement. She made a claim: He is mine now, not yours. Your spirit can suffer and for that very reason it can remember. It was Descartes' philosophy with a difference. "I suffer, therefore I am."[32]

In *Stamboul Train* the comments are more discreetly implanted in the action. Greene sets his scene and then moves in for a closer look. The narrative slows, comes to a stop, and the author intrudes. A good example is Czinner's oversimplified statement to Coral about class differences. He sounds very little like a socialist revolutionary and very much like Greene defending his own class. The scene gives way to Czinner's monlogue about his past, his duties to his people, his parents, and a God he no longer believes in. Then he makes his statement of intention: "I am not a son, he thought, nor a doctor, nor a believer, I am a Socialist," and Greene interjects, "The word mouthed by politians on innumerable platforms, printed in bad type on bad paper in endless newspapers, rang cracked."[33]

In *Brighton Rock* authorial intrusion is almost entirely contained within the narrative. When Rose sits alone in the car after Pinkie has told her to shoot herself, she wonders, "What will he do . . . if I don't . . . shoot?" Greene speculates: "Would he shoot himself alone, without her? Then he would be damned, and she wouldn't have her chance of being damned too, of showing Them they couldn't pick and choose." Rose continues: "To go on living for years . . . you couldn't tell what life would do to you." And Greene concludes: "Belief in her mind had the bright clarity of images, of the crib at Christmas: here goodness ended, past the cow and sheep, and there evil began— Herod seeking the child's birthplace from his turreted keep."[34] The monologue switches neatly from Rose to Greene, to Rose; the shift is hardly distinguishable.

But in the religious novels Greene's voice becomes more obvious again, and his comments appear as aphorisms inserted into the text. "It is astonishing the sense of innocence that goes with sin" he tells us

in *The Power and the Glory* in the middle of an anonymous confession
to the whisky priest, and earlier in the same novel:

> Man was so limited he hadn't even the ingenuity to invent a new vice: the
> animals knew as much. It was for this world that Christ had died; the
> more evil you saw and heard about you, the greater glory lay around the
> death. It was too easy to die for what was good or beautiful, for home or
> children or a civilisation—it needed a God to die for the half-hearted and
> the corrupt.[35]

In *The Heart of the Matter* we are told:

> Despair is the price one pays for setting oneself an impossible aim. It is,
> one is told, the unforgiveable sin, but it is a sin the corrupt or evil man
> never practises. He always has hope. He never reaches the freezing-point
> of knowing absolute failure. Only the man of good will carries always in
> his heart this capacity for damnation.[36]

Authorial intrusion is strong here, appearing as a Godlike voice to
mold the narrative. True, "even the author, poor devil," as Greene
once said of François Mauriac, "has a right to exist."[37] But whereas a
reader usually accepts such authorial interventions, a viewer of narrative film does not. They break into its representational reality and,
as in the adapted *Our Man in Havana*, upset its rhythm.

When we look at the frequency and method of these intrusions, we
see a far more obvious attempt to influence the reader in the Catholic
novels than appears in the earlier or later ones. This follows the
general pattern in these books of divorcing reality from material
history. Although the religious novels have the same surface realism,
empirical reality is more heavily manipulated in them, and the
tension between the individual and society, which informed the
earlier and to a large degree the later work, is shifted. We have moved
away from the world we see into the deeply personalized landscapes of
the protagonists' souls.

This is evident not only in the allegorically heightened settings
but also in the way the sequences of the novels are arranged. Believing
that "to 'establish' something is almost invariably wrong,"[38] Greene
claims never to have trusted film producers who talked to him of "the
necessity of 'establishing' this or that and the imaginary value of
'continuity.'" He says that he has always preferred to "let the reins
loose [and] the horse . . . find its way home," the shape growing from
inside the story rather than being thought out beforehand.[39] His
novels have therefore folded back on themselves in memories, diaries,

and letters and leaped ahead in dreams and other foreshadowings, life appearing as a series of incidents plucked at random which when juxtaposed produce meaning.

But although still spatially rather than temporally oriented, the religious novels are constructed to give a Catholic order to reality. Continuity in these bleakest of Greene's books is imposed through series of clues that establish their protagonists' salvation. In *The Power and the Glory* this is done through interlocking dreams, Luis's disinterest in his mother's religious stories, and the timely appearance of the new priest. In *The End of the Affair* there are Sarah's secret baptism and the miracles, which Greene eventually removed when he saw how they forced realism. Proof of sanctity is important in these books, for it is what gives flesh to the religious concepts that occupy their protagonists. But Greene was right in feeling that " 'continuity' is often the enemy of life."[40] His attempt to establish it is sometimes mechanical and, as Dmytryk noted when he removed the miracles from *The End of the Affair*, contrary to the inescapable photographic literalness of film.

Film has an obligation to representational reality that makes it very difficult to catch a world of the mind, which is precisely what Greene's religious novels do. Feelings are easily protrayed on celluloid through facial expressions. The close-up at the end of *The Third Man* of Harry Lime begging Martins to administer the coup de grâce, speaks brilliantly of every nonrational emotion in the film. But Greene's religious novels deal with concepts, the intellectual experiences of heaven and hell. In order to convey them, he has worked repesentational reality in such a way that it has become as subjective as his protagonists' monologues.

In the social novels Greene used cinematic methods of handling space and time to give deeply embedded psychological reality precise expression. He began with visible objects that he connected through juxtaposition as a film maker would, and then, by changing the point of view from which they were observed, he created ambiences that the reader accepted as real in the way a film viewer does the settings of movies. Those books gave readers (and, when adapted, viewers) a sense of the way things were as well as any books written in England in the second half of the 1930s. That is not to say that what they described was historically exact, but that they painted an extremely convincing picture of the world in which they were received.

In fact, so capable was Greene of producing settings that appeared

accurate in their documentary detail that the reader measured the
protagonist against them; that is, the characters were seen in contrast
to their ambience. Pinkie, for example, told us that he could achieve
Colleoni's success, but the setting, which we took as truth, proved
him wrong. As a film viewer does, the reader observed the subjective
against the objective and gained insight into character through the
juxtaposition. This also happens in Greene's later books written in
the first-person, only there the protagonist as well as the reader
understands himself.

But in the religious novels material reality was obfuscated to create
the deeply personalized settings of the protagonists' minds. Greene's
acumen at manipulating empirical detail in these books was remarkable, but it produced an ambience that mirrored the character, not one
against which he could be measured in this cinematic way. So the
setting lost its vitality and became a backdrop for the scene rather
than the mechanism through which character was exposed.

Yet to judge from the number of films produced in the 1950s,
directors were as enticed by the cinematic possibilities of Greene's
writing as he was by the enormous success of *The Third Man*. When
the texts or the censors posed problems, plots, settings, names,
intentions, and sometimes even the directions of stories were
changed. This does not mean that no directors took their tasks as
adapters seriously. George O'Ferrall and Edward Dmytryk certainly
did when they consulted Greene about the plot changes they would
make. And even the eminent John Ford, whose *Fugitive* rightly drew
howls of indignation from Greene and the critics, considered his
adaptation "perfect." It came out, he said, "the way I wanted it
to."[41] Ford clearly thought he had done justice to Greene, as Greene
thought he had to Shaw when he adapted *Saint Joan*. So the aesthetic
questions raised by the transformations of Greene's books in the
1950s broaden into ethical ones about adaptations in general.

The constant objective of changing a novel into a film must be to
re-create in dramatic form exactly what the author created in prose,
but we know from examining Greene's work that it is an impossible
objective. When in 1967 Greene came to write the script for *The
Comedians*, he knew this too. By then his prose offered none of the
textual problems it had during the Catholic period. The cinematic
balance between empirical and psychological reality in his work was
redressed. When once again his moral themes became tightly con-

nected to political issues, his prose became so acutely objective that in *The Quiet American*, for example, certain scenes could be taken directly from his journalism. And the novels' settings regained their highly cinematic character when they moved to the newsworthy trouble spots he began visiting in the early fifties. But although *The Comedians* was for these reasons more adaptable than the novels of the Catholic period, Greene and director Peter Glenville still chose to take liberties with the book when they turned it into a film.

They successfully incorporated long, serious passages about commitment straight from the novel and used the setting to create trememdous visual irony, but at the same time they changed the plot somewhat and shirked the demands of the original in several places. Nevertheless, like its successor film, *Travels with My Aunt*, which Greene did not script and which departed widely from the book, *The Comedians* was an interesting adaptation that carried many of his desires for common art to the screen. It evoked the intention of the original and gave a fairly accurate reflection of character so that it also fulfilled some practical objectives for adaptation. Both it and *Travels with My Aunt* showed that it is possible to change plot and even tamper to some extent with character and produce film that still bears a reasonable facsimile of the author's intention.

6
The
Visual
Image

Unlike other adaptations of Greene's work, the film made from *The Comedians* (1967) is long, intellectual, and full of the kind of complex dialogue usually reserved for the theater. But there is plenty for the camera as well, for the story is laid in Haiti, a country whose ugly politics spew up naked corruption and visible inhumanity at every turn. On this island Greene drops three innocents and a skeptical narrator to produce one of his finest novels, a black comedy that provided opportunities for everything poetic cinema should be. This is not to say that the film is flawless or that it does not depart from the novel from time to time. Elizabeth Taylor's performance as Martha ruins most of the scenes in which she appears and reductive changes are made to the story's ending. Nevertheless, *The Comedians* is an adroit adaptation in which Greene's characters bear their philosophical and political persuasions well through the camera's probing account of Haiti's violence.

Director Peter Glenville, who had staged Greene's play *The Living*

Room in 1953, introduces us to the Nightmare Republic before Brown (Richard Burton), Jones (Alec Guinness) and the Smiths (Lillian Gish and Paul Ford) arrive on the *Medea*. A children's chorus religiously chants: "Duvalier; creator of the new Haiti; President for life; idol of the masses." The picture blurs and refocuses on photographs of three dead men. They and others are tacked to the office walls of Captain Concasseur (Raymond St. Jacques), head of the Tontons Macoute. The dark glasses, obstreperous behavior, and brute strength of Papa Doc's secret police cut a forboding image across the screen. A boat whistles, and our comedians arrive in the "glassy sparkle of late sun."[1]

The customs shed is a bustle of porters, taxi drivers, police, and beggars. Jones expects to be met by a Colonel Biche but is instead incarcerated by Captain Concasseur. The Smiths look forward to combining a restful vacation with their mission to transform Haiti through vegetarianism and are confronted by begging lepers and officials who assume that Barmine and Yeastrol are illicit drugs. Brown wants only to return to his empty hotel and emptier affair with Martha. He is met by the giggling local gossip columnist, Petit Pierre, who, in hustling him into a taxi and rescuing the Smiths from customs, welcomes us all to Haiti. As the car pulls away from the harbor, it passes a sign flaunting Papa Doc's slogan: "I am the Haitian flag; I am the people." Brown mumbles, "He lives for them and they die for him."

The scene is tightly cut to produce an intensely ironic dialogue between the camera and the action. The singing, the signs, and Petit Pierre tell us one thing, the circumstances of the voyagers' arrival, quite another. The sharp visual contrast between the incredulous innocence and lack of preparation of Jones and the Smiths and the immediate and irrational evil of Haiti dramatizes Brown's suggestion in the novel's second paragraph that in coming to the republic the comedians have passed that "point of no return unremarked at the time in most lives."[2]

Greene and Glenville create a series of similar visual contrasts throughout. As in the opening sequence, the juxtapositions first involve the difference between the dictator's propaganda—the signs, the officials' statements, the seemingly calm and leisurely pace of life—and the visual information we pick up as the characters go about their business. But very quickly, from the time the body of Doctor

Philipot, Secretary for Social Welfare, is found in the pool, the ironic thrust changes to focus on the gap between what Haiti is and the way the comedians deal with it.

The technique is subtle and the impact great. The political situation in Haiti is obvious from the first, but Greene's use of it to mirror the modern world is more slowly revealed as each point is visually reinforced until there can be no question that "only the nightmares are real in this place. . . . Cruelty . . . sweeps from one spot to another."[3]

Like the Ancient Mariner, Greene holds us with his tale of horror until the comedians no longer inhabit Haiti and Petit Pierre has bid us farewell from beside the airport sign that welcomes other would-be travelers to the Nightmare Republic. Until then we are obliged to witness murder, starvation, public execution, torture, corruption, and decay. We must watch our protagonists try to hide in absurd commitments, lies, and repudiations. And we must learn with Brown that there is no escape. Everyone is involved in the brutality of Haiti because it reflects the nature of the modern world.

To bring us to this conclusion more rapidly than we reach it in the novel, Greene has rearranged the scenes so that the horror increases regularly as the film progresses. The effect attenuates the Smiths' naïveté about Haiti and moves uncommitted Jones and Brown more quickly to action. In the book, for example, the Smiths are taken to Duvalierville after they witness the disruption of Doctor Philipot's funeral. On film these incidents are reversed so that Smith meets the new minister of social welfare first and then is driven to Duvalierville; the funeral follows, allowing Mrs. Smith to vent her anger, and in close succession comes the public execution at which she collapses.

The buildup of brutality has a cumulative effect on the film's pattern of visual irony. In this instance Brown's acrid comments and the glances he shares with the minister of social welfare undercut Smith's simplicity in presenting his plans for a vegetarian center in Duvalierville. In juxtaposition with the following shots of the "model" city's broken-down buildings and the Tontons' brutality to the lepers who inhabit them, Smith's naïveté begins to appear more like simplemindedness. The funeral follows. In this sequence Mrs. Smith's spontaneous desire to help Mrs. Philipot is contrasted with the violence of the police. Smith is unmoved until Concasseur pushes his wife against the wall. At this point he too becomes physically violent and, for all his vegetarianism, has to be restrained by Brown. When we next see the Smiths, it is at the public execution. They are rushing among excited schoolchildren for an advantageous position at this "special occasion." The children's chant, "Duvalier, creator of the new Haiti," is the same one that opens the film. It is Mrs. Smith's scream above it that signals her acknowledgment of what the camera has shown us all along. When in the next sequence Smith says good-bye to Brown with, "You must find us ridiculous," the ironic dialogue we have watched between the camera and the Smith's reactions temporarily comes to a standstill.

The film's rearrangement of incidents also makes the story run chronologically. The novel often employs flashbacks—for instance, Brown's past is revealed in this way—and recalls events, like the execution and Doctor Magiot's death. In reordering the story, Greene greatly reduces dialogue and makes the incidents more visual. He also increases the number of atrocities the audience actually sees. This is in contrast to his usual cinematic style. In *The Third Man*, for example, horror was decreased by having things happen offscreen. One remembers the delicacy of that film's handling of the children's ward and of Martins's and Lime's final confrontation at the dark end of the tunnel. In *The Comedians*, along with Mrs. Smith and the schoolchildren, we are forced to watch the public execution under arc lights, the whole recorded by a television camera. Doctor Magiot's death too becomes a grizzly scene. In the novel it is related after the fact in the following manner: " . . . they sent a peasant to his door asking him to come and help a sick child. He came out on to the path and the Tontons Macoute shot him down from a car. There were witnesses. They killed the peasants too, but that was probably not intended."[4] In the film Magiot's throat is slit with his own scalpel as he pleads for time to finish the surgery he has begun.

The addition of overt violence to Greene's work may have resulted partly from the necessity of making a point quickly on the screen, but it was probably also the result of the general increase of violence in films at that time. These and similar scenes are additions to the novel and occur outside the main flow of its action. Yet they are perhaps a necessary part of a film made for viewers, most of whom, like Brown, had become so accustomed to such spectacles that they were no longer concerned by them. These scenes shock us, as they do Mrs. Smith, into recognizing that "violent deaths are natural deaths here."[5]

The new arrangement of sequences also helps Greene prepare the narrative for filming by adjusting its point of view. In *The Third Man*, Calloway told a story in which he was only peripherally involved. Although Greene's first-person novels, including *The Comedians*, probably benefited from *The Third Man* technique, on the screen protagonist Brown is too involved to narrate his own tale. The camera reveals too much of him to permit the tight control that Calloway keeps and is too fast to allow the gradual evolution of his character that the novel requires.

On paper Brown is an immensely effective narrator because he is the least involved of the comedians and the only one who knows Haiti well enough to offer a view that is at once skeptical and ironic. He is also the only entirely rootless character—Jones, after all, creates a past for himself with his lies—and thus holds the only view broad enough to "admire the dedicated, the Doctor Magiots and the Mr. Smiths for their courage and their integrity, for their fidelity to a cause," but also to resist "the temptation of sharing the security of a religious creed or a political faith, and . . . [remain] committed to the whole world of evil and of good, to the wise and the foolish, to the indifferent and to the mistaken."[6] While remembering Greene's warning that "Brown is not Greene,"[7] Brown's point of view, like that of all Greene's other first-person narrators, is very close to an omniscient author's.

On film such narration is impossible because the narrator is replaced to a great extent by the camera. Brown is still central; his role is larger than that of the other comedians, and his dialogue is essential to our understanding of them. But his role is modified. In the novel it is his black wit and irreversible skepticism that makes the Smiths' reactions ironic. On film the camera's objectivity replaces many of his comments and becomes the foil for the Smiths' innocence. The camera reveals so much that our view of things cannot be kept as closely tied to the narrator's as it is in the novel. Our firsthand observation of Jones and Martha at the embassy, for example, makes it impossible for us to share Brown's suspicions of him, which we do in the book. And watching him with Martha gives us a far more objective view of their relationship than Brown the narrator admits.

The overview of the camera also allows the story's ending to be changed. On the screen it is obvious when Brown goes off with the insurgents that both he and Jones will die. Greene's book depends on

Brown's survival. So does the story's tone, which is closely tied to the irony in Brown's acceptance of "nothing except to go on living,"[8] a choice that lands him a job in Mr. Fernandez's funeral parlor. Greene's film ending traps both Brown and Jones. It forces them to play roles to the death: it does not allow them, as the novel does, to choose these roles. Both characters thus lose stature, and the film loses a great deal of the novel's philosophic impact. Again Greene seems to have lightened his work for the cinema.

Yet there are other considerations here. The film is a long 156 minutes. To have followed the novel would have lengthened the movie by at least another 30. And although the new ending prevents the novel's ultimate irony—that Brown, who has chosen "nothing," chooses everything in deciding "to go on living"—it is well within his character to join the guerrillas.

Brown, Greene has said:

> . . . is a beachcomber-type character. . . . [he has been] washed up on the beach in Haiti, and at the end when he becomes an undertaker he has just been washed up on another shore. In the film the ending is different but the point is the same. He does not want to join the guerrillas and he has no experience in guerrilla warfare, but he makes the best of the situation.[9]

That is not quite the way the reader sees Brown who, though resigned to life at the novel's end, as Greene says, nevertheless chooses how he will live it: with no commitment to buffer the absurdity of modern existence. His choice of nothingness commits him philosophically as surely as the Smiths' vegetarianism. The film's ending denies Brown the possibility of making this decision.

Jones suffers a worse fate under the new ending, for he never has time to get tired of the roles he plays. In the book the Haitian experience turns the game serious. His last words to Brown are, "I'm going to keep it up, old man,"[10] and young Philipot reports that Jones "had found what he called a good place."[11] In Brown's final dream Jones says, "Don't ask me to find water. I can't. I'm tired, Brown, tired. After the seven hundredth performance I sometimes dry up on my lines."[12] Jones has decided to make the role of leader of the insurgents his last, and he plays it with style. "He was a wonderful man," Philipot tells Brown. "With him we began to learn, but he didn't have enough time. The men loved him. He made them laugh."[13] The film's, "Oh, I don't want to go back," is a thin substitute for Jones's decision, which, in the novel, gives him considerable stature.

Yet the new ending, with Brown standing before the cheering insurgents armed with bicycle pumps filled with gasoline and wooden clubs is, if less philosophical, an acceptable alternative. "We are crazy fools," he shouts to the rebels. "You don't know how to fight, I don't know how to fight. A painter, a hotel keeper and you—you stupid bastards—the rabble of the cockpit and the slums." Amid their cheers and young Philipot's obvious enthusiasm there is certainly the same absurdity as in the novel's notion of Brown attending at funerals. And the image of him as Jones's replacement is intensely comic.

Aside from this change in the ending, which begins when Jones and Brown wake up in the morning in the cemetery, and the change in the chronology of the sequences, there are few differences between the novel and the film. As with *Our Man in Havana*, Greene has dramatized some scenes that were recalled in the novel. For example, Jones's arrest at the beginning of the film is shown to us, whereas in the book it is described afterward. And we see him try to con the government into buying American guns rather than hear of the attempt.

Some scenes have been deleted to tighten the narrative. One is the sequence in which Jones gets himself aboard the *Medea* before he goes to Martha's embassy. In the film Greene has him leave Brown's hotel in his disguise, which saves time and achieves the same result without losing the comedy of the situation. Other sequences have been added. In the film Piñeda slaps Martha during a discussion. This is not in the novel, but it quickly adds to our understanding of their relationship. Similarly, following the cockfight on the pier, Greene gives Philipot a new speech about the blinded cock that ends with: "I believe because it is impossible. A Christian saint said that." The addition instantly defines Philipot's political position.

The adaptation of dialogue necessitated some changes. The novel is reflective and often philosophical and thus seemingly difficult to film. Greene gets around this by using the political level of the film, in which most of the visible action takes place, to carry the heavier passages. For example, Brown's quip to Smith, "You've come to a vegetarian country. Ninety-five percent of the people can't afford meat and fish," is part of the Ministry of Social Welfare sequence in the film. In the book it comes earlier, when Smith first reveals to Brown his vegetarian schemes. By moving the speech to a position where it can be contrasted with visible action, Greene saves time and increases irony. The conclusion of Doctor Magiot's letter to Brown, which expresses the core of the message, "There is always an alternative to the faith we lose,"[14] is similarly transferred. In the film it becomes part of Brown's and Philipot's discussion about Jones's future escape. Philipot speaks the lines in reply to Brown's "I have no faith in faith."

In other places the dialogue is simply shortened. In the cemetery, for example, Greene maintains the spirit of the original by quickening the audience's acceptance of Jones's confession with small additions after he has greatly shortened the scene. In the novel Brown says simply, "I like you, Jones." In the film the line is lengthened to "I always liked you, only I never knew why until now. We both came out of the same stable only you never lost your innocence." Since we identify with Brown, we quickly accept this final opinion of Jones. Brown then absolves Jones, something he does not do in the novel. The act dramatizes what he feels about Jones and enables Greene to eliminate several pages of the book's dialogue.

Greene has been able to rework the novel to advantage in another way as well. The film is long, and the incidents develop slowly in comparison to most of the films he worked on, but this is in keeping with the tone of the book and with the warm, colorful, sleepy, superficial atmosphere of the setting. Its leisurely pace makes the brutality of the real Haiti all the more vivid and enhances our feeling that "cruelty's like a searchlight. . . . We only escape it for a time."[16] In preserving the novel's pace, Greene maintains the balance of visual irony that carries the story's political impact. The slowness of the film allows him to expand his political statement about Haiti, as he does in the novel, so that the republic becomes the starting point for a discussion of the individual pursuit of happiness at a time when violence and injustice in public life seem uncontrolled.

But although *The Comedians* reaches far beyond Haiti, its immediate political statement infuriated Papa Doc's government. In a ninety-seven-page bulletin, *Graham Greene Finally Exposed*, published in 1968 by the Department of Foreign Affairs of the Republic of Haiti, the film was called "a swindle" and Greene himself "a contemner of the Negro race." Greene, Peter Glenville, and "the

countries using Graham Greene and Peter Glenville as a cover-up"
were condemned as having "committed the crime of indirect aggres-
sion against the Black Republic of Haiti." "Aren't Graham Greene's
novel *The Comedians* and Peter Glenville's film an episode of the
international plot against the Haitian Government?" the bulletin
asked. "Graham Greene thought he was going to destroy Haiti," but
"we will prove without a shade of doubt that the prosecutor has no
moral authority whatsoever, to play his part and carry out his
demolishing mission."[17]

Mentioning Greene's wartime connection with the British Secret
Service and calling him "some sort of private detective, . . . a
scrupleless [sic] and dangerous man," the pamphlet concluded with
this memorandum from the Department of Foreign Affairs, entitled,
"Reaction—Haitian Chancellerie Memorandum to Diplomats in
Haiti:"

> The Department of Foreign Affairs presents its compliments to the chiefs
> of Diplomatic Missions accredited in Haiti, and has the honor to call
> their attention to the film *The Comedians* staged by Metro Goldwyn
> Mayer, the theme of which is inspired by Graham Greene's novel of the
> same name. The shooting of this film and its showing in different
> countries constitute an act of indirect aggression against the Republic of
> Haiti. This is why it protests in the name of the Haitian government
> against the showing of this film that is considered as an act of indirect
> aggression against the Republic of Haiti. . . . The Department of Foreign
> Affairs while asking the Chiefs of the Diplomatic Missions accredited in
> Haiti to inform their respective Government, avails of this opportunity
> to assure them of its high esteem.
>
> Port-au-Prince, January 15, 1968[18]

Greene found the pamphlet so grossly outrageous that he did not
consider it seriously.[19] Nor, it seems, did the governments to whom
it was directed, for the film continued to be shown in cinemas in the
United States and Britain, and was aired on CBS Television three
years later, thus reaching an even larger audience. At that time the
Haitian embassy in Washington again denounced the film, though
in a far milder tone. It described Haiti as

> a land of smiling, singing, dancing, happy people, . . . not a country of
> crime, or witchcraft or of diabolic excesses. . . . The Haitian government
> is convinced that this television program is propaganda intended to

adversely affect tourism and its efforts to improve its economy and the lives of its people.[20]

By then Papa Doc himself had attacked Greene's book in an interview he gave in *Le Matin*, the paper he owned in Port-au-Prince. "Le livre," he said, "n'est pas bien écrit. Comme l'oeuvre d'un écrivain et d'un journaliste, le livre n'a aucune valeur" ("The book is not well written. As the work of a writer and journalist, the book has no value").[21] The government had tried to stop the film's distribution by suing Greene for £1,800,000 in libel damages in France. Haiti won the case but was awarded the insulting sum of 1 franc.[22]

Every attempt that Duvalier made to thwart the film was ineffectual. Even before Greene's novel was published, Glenville had been engaged to direct the movie and had persuaded Greene to write the script. Realising that he would never be able to shoot the film in Haiti, or even visit the country once word was out that he was to direct it, Glenville had gone there in advance of the book's release to take photographs that would later be invaluable in preparing sets. Although he had to leave the country quickly when he saw it mentioned in the *New York Times* that a film was to be made of the novel, his pictures enabled the crew to re-create the Haitian setting with great accuracy. This they did in Cotonu, Dahomey, where the terrain is similar to that of Haiti, in the countryside around Nice and in Studio St. Maurice, in Paris. Greene visited the three locations, mainly for his own satisfaction; the script he believed to be "sufficiently watertight to require no changes."[23]

He enjoyed being on the set and working with Glenville, whose quick mind he admired. "A screenwriter learns a great deal from watching the actual shooting,"[24] he says. He had often watched the filming of movies for which he wrote scripts. This time, without knowing it, he also got onto the screen in an advertising trailer showing the crew shooting the picture. He made a second appearance in the movies in 1973, when he picked up the part of an English cinema-insurance adjustor in *La Nuit Américaine* while watching François Truffaut shoot the film near Antibes. It was only after the scene in which Greene appeared had been shot that Truffaut discovered Greene was in it. More recently he appeared at the beginning and end of *A Letter to Graham Greene*, a Hungarian film about Vietnam.

The Comedians may have slightly raised political eyebrows in the

United States, for the last few feet were lopped off before it went into general circulation. Canadian and British copies maintained the original ending, in which, following Brown's speech to the guerrillas, the movie cuts to the airport, where the Piñedas prepare to leave for the United States. The final frames show Martha inside the plane. With tears in her eyes she looks out the window at the clouds over the mountains as the stewardess addresses the passengers: "You can unfasten your seat belts now. Our flying time to Miami will be one hour and ten minutes." In the version released in the United States, this scene was removed so that the film ends with the previous sequence, in which Petit Pierre stands beside the "Welcome to Haiti" sign. As Martha's plane takes off in the distance, he says, "Remember us. Remember poor Haiti."

Since the cut shortens the film by only a few minutes, it was obviously not made with time considerations in mind. The amputated sequence added a final bit of irony to the movie by leaving the viewer with the knowledge that the brutality he has seen was going on only one hour and ten minutes from the United States. And it reinforced Greene's point about American involvement in Haiti. Both film and novel fingered America's complicity in, to give but two examples, the big Cadillac dating from the days of United States aid to the poor of Haiti and the utter inappropriateness of the Smiths' vegetarian presidential ticket. The cut footage was in the same vein.

Critical opinion of the film was mixed. Dilys Powell complained about the new ending, which she said "distorted . . . this story of complex interrelationships and motives."[25] Andrew Sarris claimed that "Glenville misses every opportunity," even though "the lines are there in the script as cues for the director."[26] On the other hand, Arthur Knight called it "skillfully adapted,"[27] and Ian Christie praised its "beautiful script."[28] These varied opinions indicate a certain uneasiness about the film: it was neither undeniably excellent like *The Third Man* nor obviously mediocre like *Our Man in Havana*.

The Comedians was not a typical Greene film at all. It was far more intellectual than the successes of the 1940s. It tried to develop the complexities of the relationships and motives of its characters far beyond the level of those earlier films. Its plot contained a great deal more than a straightforward and soluble situation, for *The Comedians'* political implications extended far beyond Haiti and Papa Doc's obvious brutality. The pace of the film was leisurely and the dialogue lengthy. For such a film to succeed unquestionably, the acting would have to be flawless and the visual details exact. Neither are.

Elizabeth Taylor's performance was, as Greene says, "a mistake. She acted badly. She was badly shod." She played Martha so poorly that he now regrets he was ever consulted about her casting. She was, in fact, his choice. Sophia Loren was also considered for the part, but Greene preferred Taylor because of her successful portrait of Martha in the filmed *Who's Afraid of Virginia Woolf?* He felt his Martha to be the same type of character—which she is—but Taylor played the part with so little conviction and understanding that she did immeasurable damage to the film.[29] It is not often one can say that an actress who is on the screen only 20 of 156 minutes ruins a film, but in this case Taylor's performance comes close to it. And there are many disturbingly incongruous details in the movie, like the well-ironed clothes of the participants at the voodoo ceremony, and Martha's ill-fitting costumes. In a long, slow film, bad acting and wrong details stand out where they might go unnoticed in a faster-moving work.

Yet for all that, the movie succeeded in much of what it tried to do. It held its audience's attention while confronting it with political and philosophical truths. And it remained fairly faithful to Greene's intention for his characters. Although the film might have benefited from an ending closer to the original, the changes made were nevertheless acceptable, and the reflectiveness of Brown's character, which was brought about in the novel largely by having him narrate the story, could not have been accomplished in so short a time as the cinema allowed. *The Comedians*, then, might be called a qualified success as an adaptation.

Another film about which one could say the same is *Travels with My Aunt* (1972). This was the next movie made from one of Greene's novels and, although he does not like it, it is filled with robust energy and entertaining comedy. But unlike *The Comedians* it is a far from close transposition of the book. Although director George Cukor wanted to translate Greene faithfully, he has put very little of the novel into the movie. Maggie Smith is charming in her role, but she is not Greene's Aunt Augusta, and the story, which contains perhaps a third of the novel's scenes, is hardly close to the original plot. Yet although Cukor has shirked the demands of the original at almost every turn, Greene's idea remains. One cannot say, as one could with

The Quiet American, for example, that the film is an outright violation of the book. It is, rather, heavily truncated Greene that has become lightly successful Cukor.

The changes to the original are many. Both novel and film open at Henry's (Alec McCowen) mother's funeral. The brown coffin and Aunt Augusta's brilliant red hair stand out against the sharp black-and-white contrasts of the crematorium set. Almost immediately, then, the film begins to play with the novel. Henry's speculation about sticking oven doors is realized on the screen, so the funeral does not quite go without a hitch as it does in the book, the flowers "removed economically from the coffin, which at the touch of a button slid away from us out of sight." And Aunt Augusta's "I was present once at a premature cremation,"[30] is saved for another time.

The film takes over several sequences from the novel: the meeting with Wordsworth (Lou Gossett) in Aunt Augusta's flat, the flight to Paris, the exchange of money in the Hotel St. James and Albany (called the Albion and St. George in the film), and some scenes on the Orient Express with Tooley (Cindy Williams). But these scenes are fewer than the new sequences, and many of them have had extensive alterations. Aunt Augusta's story about Mr. Visconti (Robert Stephens), for example, is greatly reduced in the film to include only her meeting with him outside the "Messagerero." And even this snippet of the long story she tells in the novel is distorted when the camera leaves us in no doubt that she has been working in a brothel; the irony that Greene creates from Henry's innocence is lost in the film. Similarly, the search of Aunt Augusta's possessions, which in the novel takes place in her candle-lit Istanbul hotel room, is reduced to a greatly simplified customs search in the film.

From this sequence on, the movie departs completely from the book, to end on an African beach rather than in Paraguay and to become a story of Aunt Augusta's betrayal by Mr. Visconti rather than of her reunion with him. From here to the end it is impossible to find much of Greene. Mr. Visconti's wartime activities are missing. The fake Leonardo da Vinci he acquired from the Germans changes to a Modigliani bought by Mr. Dambreuse, which Aunt Augusta steals from his widow to get money for Visconti. Tooley's father, the Paraguayan scenes, and indeed the entire second part of Greene's novel have been left out of the film.

But it is the film's conclusion that Greene thinks is the worst of the

changes. In the book Aunt Augusta comes to her journey's end at
Visconti's side. " 'Perhaps travel for me was always a substitute,' "
she tells Henry. " 'I never wanted to travel as long as Mr. Visconti
was there.' " Our last glimpse of her is fixed in a photograph. She is at
a great party in her new house in Asunción. She is surrounded by the
American O'Toole and the local authorities. The Dutch, the British,
and the Nicaraguan ambassadors are present. Mr. Visconti, Henry
tells us, has corralled the entire diplomatic corps. Henry, who has
just found Wordsworth dead in the garden, calls gently to Augusta
across the dance floor, " 'Mother, Wordsworth's dead.' " Henry tells
us: "She only looked over her partner's shoulder and said, 'Yes, dear,
all in good time, but can't you see that now I'm dancing with Mr.
Visconti?' A flash-bulb broke the shadows up. I have the photograph
still—all three of us are petrified by the lightning flash into a family
group."[31] "I thought," Greene says, "that the two old people could
live their lives out there together."[32]

George Cukor and his scriptwriters thought differently. Their
Aunt Augusta is swindled by Visconti and left with Henry, who,
having learned a little dishonesty himself, has kept most of the
money he got from selling Dambreuse's painting. "I like you,
mother," he tells her. "But I'm not a thief. We'll buy the painting
back." "Oh," she says. "But you can't go back to the dreary dahlias."
"I'll toss you for it," Henry replies, and throws a coin high into the
air. As it turns and falls, the film slows and then freezes on their faces
looking up at it against the blue sky.

Jay Allen, one of the film's several scriptwriters and one of the two,
with Hugh Wheeler, listed in its credits, says that the movie was a
product of "bad times in the business, budget problems, fear and
funk." The rights were "bought as a project for George Cukor to do
with Katharine Hepburn, . . . and both of them were determined to
do a screen version that was, in essence, very faithful to the book."
The first screenwriter engaged was Wheeler, Allen was the second,
and Hepburn herself did two versions of the script. As Aunt Augusta,
however, Hepburn was replaced by Maggie Smith, and the movie
continued on a low budget, being filmed in Madrid, "where," Allen
says, "*all* of the travels take place. From the east of town to the west of
town." It was "shot on an eight-week schedule (four weeks under any
normal schedule for a first class production). Mr. Greene's hands are
clean," Allen adds. "He never touched the thing."[33] And Greene is
happy not to have done so, for he too regrets the film.

Yet if we look at it with more detachment, we see that it is far from being a failed movie. It is a good comedy highlighted by some rather touching scenes. Clearly Smith's Aunt Augusta is too high strung and facetious to be Greene's, but she is an amusing character in her own right, and Henry, though greatly simplified—owing in part, as was the case with Brown in *The Comedians*, to the loss of him as narrator—is nonetheless a suitable companion for her quixotic travels. Even the drastically reduced ending is not unacceptable, given Aunt Augusta's altered character. It helps turn the story into the lighter comedy it becomes on the screen by finally separating her from Visconti, who is seen, as he is in the book as well, the more dishonest of the two. Of course, the delicacies of his character are entirely lost.

The question, however, is not whether *Travels with My Aunt* is a good or bad film but what the public will accept as adaptation. The movies have always borrowed plots from books. Recent estimates of the total number of films taken from novels alone is over 50 percent. And the number of adaptations is rising.[34] Indeed, as in the instance of *The Comedians*, the film rights to many novels are sold even before the book is published, and still others, like *The Third Man*, are written for the cinema to become best sellers only after they have appeared on the screen. Viewers are well used to these practices, and also to the complaints of writers and readers when they find their own work or their favorite story somehow unsatisfactorily transposed.

But what are those complaints about? Critics perhaps worry over subtleties of technique or theory. Authors point out misconstrued intentions and arrogant deletions. Viewers, by and large, concern themselves only with content. But whether critics, authors or reader-viewers, we come to an adaptation with its meaning already firmly sunk into us. The characters are old friends, and when we give ourselves over to the cinema's enveloping control in this instance, we want the story to be as we know it. Inconsistencies jolt us out of the world we have chosen to put ourselves into for a couple of hours. We do not want what was on the page constantly challenged by what we see on the screen. We want it reinforced with all the immediacy and intensity that the cinema offers.

Taking this into consideration and looking back over the adaptations that have been made of Greene's work, we see that those that most satisfied him are those that most resemble the original. He liked *Confidential Agent* because it followed the book closely. He stood behind the script for *Brighton Rock* because of its faithfulness to his novel. He favored *The Comedians* and *England Made Me* (1973) for the same reason. *England Made Me* succeeded *Travels with My Aunt*. It was made from his early novel about Anthony and Kate Farrant and Kate's Swedish employer-lover, Eric Krogh. The work was very much socially oriented, but its concern with the rapaciousness of prewar capitalism was of less interest to today's viewer than it had been to Greene's readers in 1935. Director Peter Duffell changed the political direction of the story somewhat by resetting it in Nazi Germany. That did not disturb Greene in the least because of the film's faithfulness to his novel's intention, that is, to what he had in mind for his characters. Michael York and Hildegard Neil played a convincing Anthony and Kate, he thought, and Peter Finch gave a sympathetic performance as Eric Krogh.[35]

Such plot changes are common in adaptations, and we accept them easily, especially if they come after we have once again identified with the characters we know. If we are first allowed to do this, we will even swallow such a radical alteration as that made to the end of *The Comedians*. Scenes may be reordered as in *The End of the Affair*, passages differently stated like the one concluding *Brighton Rock*, pieces added like the bathroom sequence in *Our Man in Havana*, and peripheral characters and whole chapters removed as in *Travels with My Aunt*. If the film is brilliant in its own right, we will even forgo the pleasure of the original and delight in a new twist to the story. This we do gladly when we watch *The Fallen Idol*. But we will not accept total distortions of the author's intention, as *The Fugitive* and *The Quiet American* were, and we object strenuously to unsuitable casting unless the acting has a brilliance and cohesiveness of its own that carries us into a redefinition of the role. To some extent Maggie Smith does this as Aunt Augusta. In general, the plot may change as long as the characters do not.

The real problem is that we accept these changes too easily as memory gives way to fantasy. The movies have created myths for us about history, and they do the same on a smaller scale about the stories from which they are made. Although Greene was right when he quenched his anger about the film made from *The Quiet American*, saying only that the book would outlive the movie, adaptations do change viewers' perceptions of novels. The relationship between books and even good adaptations is not straightforward.

For viewers unfamiliar with the original, the adaptation *is* the novel. And the memories of viewers who know books well can be tricked by the movies into believing the original to be somewhat different from what it is. The cinema has a way of destroying the remembered past, and even viewers who constantly remind themselves that the simulacrum they watch is another creation, not the work from which it was taken, may confuse the two entities. The book's scenes tend to become fixed as the film defines them, and its characters are irrevocably imagined as looking like the actors who play the parts. This even happens to the author, it seems, for Greene says that he always imagines Major Calloway as Trevor Howard.[36] Sometimes the film improves the original, but that was not the case with most of Greene's adapted work, and the more limited version of it that appeared on the screen will nevertheless probably have supplanted the original in the memory of the average viewer.

This being the case, the whole process of transposing fiction becomes a weighty task. British television is famous for dramatizing novels. The secret seems to be a combination of imaginative scripting, excellent acting, magnificent costuming and setting, careful camerawork, and precise editing. The recent adaptations of Dickens, Tolstoy and Trollope, to mention only a few writers, are almost page-perfect. They give one the impression that not only the director and scriptwriter but every technician, everyone who has touched the celluloid, knows by heart each scene of the story and understands each character. In comparison, most of the transpositions of Greene's work seem woefully inadequate. Yet when we look back to *Brighton Rock*, *The Fallen Idol* and even *The Comedians*, it is easy to see how valuable those adaptations have been. All of them have been more than mere literal translations. In them Greene has retold the stories anew in a way particular to the screen.

When comparing television and film adaptations, one must also consider the problem of time. It is one thing to take a novel and serialize it for television and quite another to reduce it to cinema length. Greene's work was first adapted for television in 1959, when the BBC turned *The Third Man* into a series of successful programs, which, with the exception of Karas's music, had little to do with the original story. Harry Lime (Michael Rennie) was a slick private investigator whose life was opulent and glossy. He valued money most and surrounded himself with butlers and expensive paintings at home, women, and cosmopolitan glitter at work. In 1960 Greene's play *The Complaisant Lover* was adapted by the BBC, and in 1961, *The Power and the Glory*, by CBS. The latter film was of some interest because Laurence Olivier played the priest, and it was thus given a limited cinema showing in Britain. It was closer to the novel than John Ford's *The Fugitive* but was not completely successful because it deleted the appearance of the new priest at the story's end. And in 1963 the BBC adapted *Stamboul Train*, which Greene says was worse than the film.

These early television reworkings were either commercialized Greene or films that suffered the same condensation problems as cinema productions. In 1976, however, Thames Television adapted eighteen of Greene's stories for a series entitled, *Shades of Greene*. Like *The Fallen Idol*, which is a rich example of the possibilities in transposing short pieces, these dramas were highly successful. Among Greene's favorites are *Dream of a Stange Land, Blue Film, Under the Garden, The Destructors, Alas Poor Mailing*, and *Two Gentle People*. He found the casting astute and the acting excellent.[37] The series, which included performances by Paul Scofield, Roy Kinnear, Virginia McKenna, Ian Hendry, John Gielgud, and Donald Pleasence, ranged from humorous epigrams to full-length dramas. The films evoked the intention and atmosphere of Greene's stories with faithfulness and charm and combined to make a successful drama series.

Adaptation of full-length novels for the cinema, however, requires things to move so quickly that such intricate transpositions cannot generally be expected. Nevertheless, Greene's work is getting careful treatment these days. When Tom Stoppard wrote the script for *The Human Factor* (1980), he consulted Greene several times, which is a far cry from the way many scriptwriters of the earlier novels went about their work. The film is a very close adaptation of the novel, perhaps too faithful for Greene, who remains dissatisfied with his book. "They needn't have stuck so closely to the original,"[38] he says.

His ambition after the war was to write an espionage story free of violence, which, "in spite of James Bond, [had not] been a feature of the British Secret Service."[39] But his novel *The Human Factor* went its own way and had in it Davis's death. And Doctor Percival, Greene felt, was not a typical figure of the service. Perhaps not, but he is an interesting fictional character, and played by Robert Morley, he becomes the center of some of the film's more memorable scenes. It was "as a love story—a married-love story of an elderly man"[40] that Greene thought the novel succeeded. But it is here that the film is unsatisfying. Even the fine acting of Nicol Williamson as Castle and the support he gets from Derek Jacobi as Davis, Richard Attenborough as Daintry, and John Gielgud as Tomlinson, cannot erase the error at the center of the film created by Iman's colorless performance as Sarah. And one misses the novel's details, the names of real places, clubs, and streets, that give Greene's writing the documentary look we are accustomed to.

Stoppard has caught the book's humdrum tone, and Greene's voice is echoed in the carefully transposed dialogue and in the characters themselves. Indeed, with the exception of the final sequence, which is shot on an unconvincing studio set of Castle's Moscow apartment, the film is very good adaptation. Yet as a movie it is unsatisfying. The main problem is Iman's shortcomings as an actress. But Greene's Sarah is also flat. For the film to succeed, Stoppard would have had to flesh her out more than Greene did in his novel. Also, the pace is rather slow for the average viewer of spy stories. Greene's intention was to challenge the James Bond myth, but does such a good yet sad man as Castle in such a slow film as *The Human Factor* hold an audience's attention long enough to do this?

In the novel Greene's writing is as tight and subtly ironic as it has ever been, the sequences are as incisively cut, and the dialogue as economical. His shaping and telling of the story, the way he organizes the plot, and his method of producing atmosphere lend this book the same cinematic look that distinguishes everything he writes. Yet even Stoppard's careful transposition of these novelist's talents did not produce excellent cinema.

The latest of the films, made from *The Honorary Consul*, the novel Greene now prefers over all his others, is notable only as an example of how not to adapt fiction. Named *Beyond the Limit* in America, it is composed of a large number of establishing shots, the kind Greene insisted had no place in novels and films, and flat sequences that fail to show Plarr as the entirely uncommitted doctor he is in the novel. Innumerable car rides, usually so tightly framed as to exclude the all-important background, show movement from one scene to another; a brief dinner sequence establishes the hostess, whom we never see again, as the police chief's mistress; the opening frames are supposed to introduce us to the English Club but fail to mention its name.

Worse is the exclusion of detail, which in the novel is largely contained in dialogue. Greene uses Clara's first visit to Plarr's flat to build character: she has become a prostitute to support her family. Because she has never been in an elevator, Plarr holds her hand protectively. He offers her juice, but she does not like juice and takes coffee. These and similar bits of dialogue could easily fill the silent gaps in the film and give substance to what, in this case, becomes the first of too many contrived sex scenes.

Later in the hut the sunglasses that Plarr has bought Clara are placed beside Charley's bed. The shot of them passes without comment. Plarr's statement in the novel—"Clara—I paid her with a pair of sunglasses"—should have been used to reinforce their presence, but the script misses the line, as we do the sunglasses. More important, Dr. Saavedra has been left out of the film; Leon's and Plarr's conversations, which hold the philosophical crux of the novel, are deleted, and the political intention, which is similar to that of *The Comedians*, has not survived.

Greene is not discouraged however, and he says he is more realistic about what to expect from adaptations of his work than he used to be. As well, things have changed somewhat since he first wrote for the movies. In the old days scriptwriters were often just regular employees of the business. The rights were bought, and books were turned over to them to be adapted with little or no consultation with the novelist. Of course, when a novelist of Greene's stature was hired, he was usually asked personally by the director to do a certain script. But even then the script was often changed without his knowledge, and sometimes a perfectly good screenplay was ruined by carelessness when it was turned into the shooting script. This final transition is something Greene thinks an author cannot do, except in conjunction with the director. He did it alone for *Brighton Rock* but was uneasy with the task. It is better done jointly, he thinks.

Today most directors and scriptwriters who adapt his work keep in touch with him even though he is not formally a member of the film team. As of this writing, Lindsay Hogg is adapting *Doctor Fischer of Geneva*. He, Greene, and producer Richard Broke worked out a scenario without dialogue together from which Broke finished the job. Greene thinks it reads well and has been on location in Switzerland to watch some of the filming.[41] And he still hopes that someone will put *It's a Battlefield* on the screen. This novel has always seemed obviously cinematic to him because of the way its scenes are cut. There is also *The Living Room*, for which Greene wrote a script some years ago. "Various producers have tried to arrange production but always failed with the big distributing companies. . . . On two different occasions Mr. Michael Powell [a director of Holborn Productions Limited] has been on the verge of setting it up, and was let down at the last minute."[42] In 1970, Athene Seyler and Nigel Davenport were engaged to act in it, but at the moment, the film is not being considered for production. More recently Greene agreed to adapt Joseph Conrad's *The Secret Agent* for Joseph Losey but lost interest when the American producer tried to get him to work with another director.[43] The story "May We Borrow Your Husband?" was at one time worked on by Dimitri Tiomkin and may still reach the screen. And MGM is reconsidering making a film of *The Tenth Man*.

Greene does not now go to the movies as often as he used to, but he does watch television and sees the adaptations of his work shown on it. The cinema is still of great interest to him, and since it appears that he will continue to be involved, whether or not he actually writes scripts for films of his work, we can look forward to more careful transpositions like *England Made Me* and *The Human Factor*. One hopes, of course, that he will again dramatize his own writing, for though not all his scripts have made excellent films, they have done what good adaptations should do: they have retold the story faithfully while making comments particular to their new form.

Graham Greene on the set of *The Comedians,* 1967. Courtesy of The Museum of Modern Art, Film Stills Archive.

Richard Burton on the set of *The Comedians*, 1967. Courtesy of The Museum of Modern Art, Film Stills Archive.

Alec Guinness as Major Jones in *The Comedians,* 1967. Courtesy of The Museum of Modern Art, Film Stills Archive.

7

Greene
Sums Up

The High Street in Berkhamstead where Graham Greene walked as
a child "was wide as many a market square, but its broad dignity was
abused after the first great war by the New Cinema under a green
Moorish dome, tiny enough but it seemed to us then the height of
pretentious luxury and dubious taste." Greene's father, "who was by
that time headmaster of Berkhamstead School, once allowed his
senior boys to go there for a special performance of the first *Tarzan*
movie, under the false impression that it was an educational film of
anthropological interest, and ever after he regarded the cinema with a
sense of disillusion and suspicion."[1] But the young Greene, who first
went to the movies in Brighton at the age of six, took no heed of his
father's disappointing experience. The film he saw was an adaptation
of Anthony Hope's *Sophie of Kravonia*, and the story captured him
forever. It was "the kind of book I always wanted to write," he says,
"the high romantic tale, capturing us in youth with hopes that prove
illusions, to which we return again in age in order to escape the sad
reality."[2]

If the story captured him forever, so did the movies. He took them seriously from the first because they were a popular art, the precise reason many intellectuals did not. But his early hopes for the cinema were not borne out by his practical experience. Like so many other artists, he was forced to make aesthetic concessions throughout his career to censors and budgets and inept decisions by film executives.

But more maddening to him as a novelist was the loss of control he experienced to the machinery of the film process. It was a pretty distressing business for a writer's part in making films is relatively small. He often felt "bewildered . . . watching the rough cut, clearing his throat nervously at new lines that are not his, feeling a sense of guilt because he was the only spectator who remembers what happened once—like a man who has witnessed a crime and is afraid to speak, an accomplice after the fact."[3] "The film producer," he quickly came to realize, "can alter anything. He can turn your tragedy of East End Jewery into a musical comedy at Palm Springs if he wishes. . . . irony can be turned into sentiment by some romantic boob of an actor. . . . Even if a script be followed word by word there are those gaps of silence which can be filled with the banal embrace."[4]

"Look at what Elizabeth Taylor made of *The Comedians*," Greene recently commented:

> She even insisted on doing her own clothes. We had to pay her way because of Burton so I thought, well, Martha's a short part, maybe she can do it. I had seen her in Albee's *Who's Afraid of Virginia Woolf*. And in *Our Man in Havana* Guinness took the rap from the critics, but the fault wasn't his. It was Jo Morrow's, who played Milly. All the scenes Morrow was in were bad. She just couldn't act. It's very frustrating for a novelist who's used to having complete control. The scratched record at the end of *Brighton Rock* was my idea. I figured those who need a happy ending will have it, and anyone with any sense will know Rose will play it again and hear the worst. Then the effect was erased on the set when Boulting panned up to the crucifix. I was in Africa. Of course, to a novelist, his novel is the best he can do with a particular subject. He will always resent many of the changes necessary for turning it into a film.[5]

Greene himself often resented those changes bitterly, though he nevertheless persisted in writing scripts. "The fact remains—one must try every drink once,"[6] he says. So, although writing novels has been his vocation since he was nineteen, the other work was of interest too, "just to see if one could do it."[7] Writing for the movies meant working for a mass audience:

I wasn't consciously aware of it when I was writing. I always wrote my films and novels to please myself, but the film audience was obviously different from that for my books. I was interested in popular art. I wrote about it in my reviews. I don't remember trying to *inform* the audience in my films, but I did try to direct film makers in my criticism.[8]

In 1928 he had found "the average film . . . irregular, thoughtless, . . . a muddled battle of impressions."[9] By 1935, when he became a film critic, he had "almost given up hope of hearing *words* with a vivid enough imagery to convey the climate of the drama."[10] Since he believed it easier to make films than to write because he felt pictures to be more exact than the prose of most of his contemporaries, and since he felt the cinema of that time to be in need of something to say, he decided that writers and films could be of use to each other. Film should have "a special interest to the writer," he thought. "The cinema needed him: pictures required words as well as images."[11]

And so as film critic he bullied, cajoled, and challenged his contemporaries to turn the movies into a truly common art. When things went wrong, he seldom blamed individuals as he often does now that he is a veteran of the business. He found fault instead with the way commercial films are made. "A film actor," he wrote, "is hardly aware of what happens when he is not on the set." He does not get a picture of the entire film as actors in the theatre where they are "interested not only in their own parts but in the play as a whole."[12] Documentary films he thought were made in a better way than were commercial movies. A documentary was "more than mere communication of fact; it was interpretation, persuasion."[13] It was a "document[of] the creator's mind"[14] because the writer–film maker maintained control of his own work. And documentaries were produced away from the large money of the commercial business, a system he still believes to be safer for the making of films.[15] "Privilege separates," he said, "and we can't afford to live away from the source of our writing in however confortable an exile."[16] If the movies were to be a popular art, the writer would have to touch the masses and use the initial group response to lead the individual to a richer understanding of himself and his world. An artist's critical faculty could not help being blunted by the film maker's bonanza. The documentary method, on the other hand, produced "the most important films being made in England,"[17] Greene thought as a film critic.

Yet, with the exception of a few wartime commentaries, all of his

own work for the film was within the entertainment trade.
Documentaries he knew were outside the mainstream of cinema. And
as novelist what he had to offer was his ability to popularize fiction.
Besides, the "glittering prizes"[18] that film work offered enabled him
to go on writing books, though he was no prostitute to the business
and refused to write for it when he found the task incompatible with
his own aesthetic values.

So, although as critic he deplored the artistic results of a novelist's
involvement with the high finance of commercial moviemaking, as
young novelist he was happy for the financial rewards it offered. And
he enjoyed the remuneration he got from other kinds of writing as
well. Rapportage afforded him travel. "Without it I could never have
gone where I did," he says. "I could not have spent five years in
Vietnam. My rapportage made travel possible. But there too I wrote
to suit myself; I never thought of the reader as anyone special; I just
wrote what I saw to please myself."[19] As a journalist pleasing himself
meant seeking out individual situations and stories within whatever
political context to draw attention to the plight of the people he
encountered. "It was obvious where I stood politically," he says.
"But I always wanted to see the other side as well. It was a documentary approach. I wanted to see the human being. I described pictures
of what I saw to set the scene for the human being."[20]

This is what he had earlier wanted the camera to do because it
could note more exactly and vividly than the prose of most of his
contemporaries the atmosphere of a story. Accuracy of setting gave
the narrative authenticity. When we recognize the truth of the
general scene, he believed, we are more prepared to accept the truth
of the individual drama.

And that is what Greene still wants in rapportage, in movies, and
in novels. He says:

> I can't stand reading books that open with descriptions of characters.
> So-and-so had red hair; someone else had blue eyes; the other was tall;
> another, thin; the redhead was this and that—after four pages I know
> nothing. I always notice this in badly written books. One wants to be
> able to *know* a character, doesn't one? We know him by what he does. If
> you don't see characters from various sides, then the characters are thin. I
> object to Forster's characters because they are too one-sided; even Virgi-
> nia Woolf's. I mean, I know Regent Street better than Mrs. Dalloway.
>   When I write I try to see every movement of the characters. Even

though I don't include all that on the page, I *see* it all. The scene plays itself out before me and I watch what the characters do. I select the essence and write it down. It's very tiring; I get eyestrain from watching them; that's why I like to sleep after lunch. The important thing is to see them from various sides. When I was writing *The Quiet American*, I found the journalist, Granger, becoming unreal. One wanted to see him as a human being, so I gave him a child back home. Some of my characters don't come alive. Wilson in *The Heart of the Matter* never did. It leaves a dead point in the book.[21]

One of the methods Greene uses to examine his characters from various sides is to slow the narrative, as a close-up does a moving picture, and look at them at close quarters. This he does in the railway shed in *Stamboul Train*, for example, or in the cemetery scene in *The Comedians*. The method reaches its climax in *The Honorary Consul*, where almost the whole story is contained in a hut, and in *Monsignor Quixote*, where much of the action takes place in Father Quixote's Seat, Rosinante. Greene adds the same kind of dramatic emphasis to his rapportage by zeroing in on particular situations to draw attention to the individual. It is a method he got from film, he says: "I think of a scene where so-and-so comes alive. It halts the story momentarily so I can watch my characters."[22]

In these enclosed spaces he shows them to us at close range. With few exceptions their features are not described, and when they are, it is usually to exaggerate one aspect of them that becomes as much a part of the character's psychological as of his physical makeup. We will never forget the mestizo's yellow teeth, for example, or Father Thomas's nose. What we have instead are the particulars of the setting, enough of them, that is, to give us the atmosphere surrounding the characters. Like a movie camera Greene catches the feeling of the individual going about his business in a particular place. What the reader does is what a viewer does at the movies: he looks about the scene to catch the overall effect, for it is through the ambience that the character comes off the page.

"I don't describe things as some critics say I do," Greene believes. "I watch. My descriptions are like what a moving camera would see. It's as though I am sitting in a car with a notebook and the car stops for a moment. Then I drive on and the view changes. In *Monsignor Quixote* this happens when they see the hammer and sickle on the wall."[23] There he wrote:

They drove very slowly, looking out for a tree which would give them shade, for the late sun was slanting low across the fields, driving the shadows into patches far too thin for two men to sit in them at ease. Finally, under the ruined wall of an outhouse which belonged to an abandoned farm, they found what they needed. Someone had painted a hammer and sickle crudely in red upon the crumbling stone.

"I would have preferred a cross," Father Quixote said, "to eat under."[24]

This shift is executed with great fluidity. As if in successive film shots the scene changes from late afternoon to dusk, from inside the car to beside the wall, from driving to sitting, and from concentrated silence to religious and political argument. The movement is entirely occasioned by the hammer and sickle.

Greene adds:

I use dialogue to change the point of view too. A character will say something to show something else. It shifts the focus; it's done like this in the movies of course, but one doesn't think about these things when one's writing. Writing is such an unconscious act. And Dickens shifted attention like this too, though I see that I've been influenced by the film in the way the Victorian novelists, especially Scott, were influenced by painting. Their settings were descriptions of paintings; mine are from a moving camera.[25]

The result, as Julian Symons has pointed out,[26] is not literal realism. If it were, it would be far easier to put on the screen. What we have are fragments of reality enlarged by the imagination in the way particulars in a close shot are lent significance beyond what they actually possess. Greene's scenes appear as visual snatches or memories, complete in themselves, that combine as film sequences do, to give us a final understanding of a period in the protagonist's life. In them things happen simultaneously, compressing time into a multi-layered image. Greene has always distrusted the A-to-Z approach in narrative because he finds it unrealistic. It is by scenes, with their emphasis on space, not time, their meaning derived from a nebula of details, not a linear progression from point to point, that Greene's characters move.

This is, of course, how films proceed, each segment of celluloid having several layers of activity that are captured through camera angles, changes in depth of focus, and so on. In Federico Fellini's *Amarcord*, for example, in the scene where the town watches a new truckload of prostitutes arrive, Fellini films several depths of field simultaneously. In the foreground is the truckload of women, in the middleground is the resident whore, and in the background are the village men, young and old. Each of these depths is used to make a different point, and the action between them creates several levels of irony. At the same time, Fellini moves his camera in a long dolly shot, cutting across the three levels of interpretation and adding a fourth. The scene explodes into meaning as its separate parts are juxtaposed in different combinations and then settles into a multi-faceted image that informs us about the characters involved.

Time and again Greene does the same thing with words, but rarely does the full impact of them reach the screen. When translated into film images, they seem to remain as separate parts instead of coming together in the explosive way Fellini's images do. In *The Fallen Idol* our understanding of Baines's predicament in the tea shop is different after we read of the tea cakes and the slab of sausage, as our view of the coming of the prostitutes is changed by Fellini's depth of field. In both scenes the separate parts come together in our minds as they do in real life, and we see, hear, touch, taste, and smell the images. In each there is an organic unity that seems to be lost in the direct realistic translation of Greene's work for the screen.

Here his adapters face an interesting problem. In losing the aesthetic unity of the scene, they lose, to a greater or lesser extent depending on the novel, the depth of characterization. Greene is right in saying that he does not describe his people. He shows us what they do, and the many layers of their behavior are held together, as they are in a cinematic sequence, by the imagery of the unit. The characters move within the scene, but the psychological and sociological motivations for their acts are suspended in its imagery, which in the religious books is so dense that one must stand back from it, as one does from an impressionist painting, to see the effect. This does not mean the image lacks exactness; it is most often deadly accurate. But it is in the overall brilliance rather than the coherence of the individual parts that we find its fidelity, and that brilliance is what film makers have had difficulty catching.

So if Greene considers only his work, it is easy to understand why he believes adaptations to be in general a poor idea. Yet having said this, he remains curious about the film process. "Why can't they adapt my work? Why can't they get it on the screen?" he wants to know. "Especially since, though I never thought of my writing as particularly cinematic except in *It's a Battlefield*, where the scenes are obviously cut that way, I see that many of the methods I use are like the film; and some of them I got from it."[27]

Evelyn Waugh also thought Greene used cinematic methods in his writing. He said, in discussing Greene's style:

> It is as though out of an infinite length of film, sequences had been cut which, assembled, comprised an experience which is the reader's alone, without any correspondence to the experience of the protagonists. The writer has become director and producer. Indeed, the affinity to the film is everywhere apparent. It is the camera's eye which moves from the hotel balcony to the street below, picks out the policeman, follows him to his office, moves about the room from the handcuffs on the wall to the broken rosary in the drawer, recording significant detail. It is the modern way of telling a story. In Elizabethan drama one can usually discern an artistic sense formed on the dumb-show and masque. In Henry James's novels scene after scene evolves as though on the stage of a drawing-room comedy. Now it is the cinema which has taught us a new habit of narrative.[28]

But although Greene, like many modern writers, borrowed some film techniques for his books, he is nevertheless a novelist, with literary traditions. In discussing the origins of montage and the close-up among various film methods, Griffith and Eisenstein acknowledged their debt to Dickens. But other writers also achieved unusual and seemingly cinematic effects before film, and by the time sound was added to moving pictures and the novelist's talents became necessary to the cinema, the most obviously filmlike novels had been written. By then all of Marcel Proust's work had appeared, and James Joyce's *Ulysses* had been published. The whole of Henry James, whose aim was to avoid explaining things by showing his reader everything, had been printed, as had all of Joseph Conrad, who insisted that he was trying to make the reader see. So if Greene honed his fiction on some film techniques, he, and indeed the film itself, drew more heavily on a literary tradition that increasingly concerned itself with the visual qualities of the novel.

With this in mind Greene's question is even more salient. Since like his literary predecessors he emphasized the reader's being able to *see* the story, and since his prose achieved a highly visual quality by taking some of its direction from film, why has it been so difficult for film makers to transfer his novels to the screen? Perhaps Greene himself gave the best answer years ago, when he was a film critic. "If you are using words in one craft," he wrote then, "it is impossible not to corrupt them by employing them in another medium . . . (Proust found even conversation dangerous—the more intelligent the more dangerous 'since it falsifies the life of the mind by getting mixed up in it')."[29]

From the adaptations of Greene's work we have seen that to call writing cinematic is of questionable use, for the printed image is entirely different from the filmed one. In discussing adaptation, one must begin with the problem of dramatizing the written image, but one must do so aware that the image will lose its integrity in transposition. What one wants from adaptation is "a true reflection of character," Greene says, but how one gets it must be left to the film maker's imagination: "One must allow that anything be changed so long as the characters come out whole."[30] And one must realize that just because fiction appears visual does not mean that it will therefore adapt easily; the printed metaphor will always be corrupted when it is turned into the visual image.

But this is perhaps the most interesting thing about adaptation. When Greene first became involved with films, he believed that novelists could turn the movies into a truly popular art. His own work with them has added two classics to British film and left us with a body of pertinent critical ideas. It has also allowed him to polish his fiction. The popularity of adaptations alone decrees that film makers will spend a good deal of their time in the future working from literary sources. As Greene picked up cinematic methods to strengthen his novels, film makers will have to stretch cinematic conventions to accommodate the literature they transpose. So in the long run the writer may be more important to the cinema than Greene first suspected, for aside from the enormous social benefits we gain in having literary texts transferred to the screen, the challenge to cinematic conventions posed by serious adaptation may prove as valuable to the movies as the movies have been to the novels of Graham Greene.

Appendix

The Films of
Graham Greene

1933　*Orient Express* (Twentieth Century-Fox)

Director: Paul Martin
Producer: Paul Martin
Script: Paul Martin, W. Conselman, Carl Hovey, Oscar Levant
Origin: Graham Greene's novel *Stamboul Train*
Cast: Heather Angel, Norman Foster, Ralph Morgan
Running time: 73 minutes

1937　*The Future's in the Air* (Strand Film Company)

Director: Alexander Shaw
Producer: Paul Rotha
Commentary: Graham Greene and Paul Rotha
Running time: 12 minutes

1940   *Twenty one Days* (Columbia Pictures)

Director: Basil Dean
Producer: Basil Dean
Script: Graham Greene and Basil Dean
Origin: John Galsworthy's play *The First and the Last*
Cast: Vivien Leigh, Laurence Olivier
Running time: 75 minutes

1940   *The Green Cockatoo* (New World Pictures) (reissued as *Race Gang* in 1953)

Director: William Cameron Menzies
Producer: William K. Howard
Scenario: Graham Greene
Script: E. O. Berkman
Origin: Original story by Graham Greene
Cast: John Mills, Rene Ray, Robert Newton
Running time: 65 minutes

1940   *The New Britain* (Strand Film Company)

Director: Ralph Keene
Producer: Alexander Shaw
Script: Reg Groves
Commentary: Graham Greene
Running time: 10 minutes

1942   *Went the Day Well?* (U.S. title *48 Hours*) (Ealing Studios)

Director: Alberto Cavalcanti
Producer: Michael Balcon
Script: John Dighton, Diana Morgan, Angus MacPhail
Origin: Graham Greene's story "The Lieutenant Died Last"
Cast: Leslie Banks, Basil Sydney, Frank Lawton
Running time: 92 minutes

1942   *This Gun for Hire* (Paramount Pictures)

Director: Frank Tuttle
Producer: Richard Blumenthal
Script: Albert Maltz, W. R. Burnett
Origin: Graham Greene's novel *A Gun for Sale*
Cast: Veronica Lake, Robert Preston, Alan Ladd
Running time: 81 minutes

1944   *Ministry of Fear* (Paramount Pictures)

> Director: Fritz Lang
> Producer: Seton Miller
> Script: Seton Miller
> Origin: Graham Greene's novel *The Ministry of Fear*
> Cast: Ray Milland, Marjorie Reynolds, Dan Duryea
> Running time: 87 minutes

1945   *Confidential Agent* (Warner Brothers)

> Director: Herman Shumlin
> Producer: Robert Buckner
> Script: Robert Buckner
> Origin: Graham Greene's novel *The Confidential Agent*
> Cast: Charles Boyer, Lauren Bacall, Katina Paxinou, Peter Lorre
> Running time: 117 minutes

1947   *The Man Within* (U.S. title *The Smugglers*) (J. Arthur Rank, Eagle Lion Films)

> Director: Bernard Knowles
> Producers: Muriel and Sydney Box
> Script: Muriel and Sydney Box
> Origin: Graham Greene's novel *The Man Within*
> Cast: Richard Attenborough, Michael Redgrave, Jean Kent
> Running time: 88 minutes

1947   *Brighton Rock* (Associated British Pictures)

> Director: John Boulting
> Producer: Roy Boulting
> Script: Graham Greene and Terence Rattigan
> Origin: Graham Greene's novel *Brighton Rock*
> Cast: Richard Attenborough, Hermione Baddeley, William Hartnell
> Running time: 92 minutes

1947   *The Fugitive* (RKO, Argosy Films)

> Director: John Ford
> Producer: Merian Cooper and John Ford
> Script: Dudley Nichols
> Origin: Graham Greene's novel *The Power and the Glory*
> Cast: Henry Fonda, Dolores Del Rio
> Running time: 104 minutes

1948   *The Fallen Idol* (London Films)

Director: Carol Reed
Producer: Carol Reed
Script: Graham Greene
Origin: Graham Greene's story "The Basement Room"
Cast: Ralph Richardson, Michèle Morgan, Sonia Dresdel, Bobby
    Henrey
Running time: 94 minutes

1949   *The Third Man* (London Films)

Director: Carol Reed
Producer: Carol Reed
Associate Producer: Hugh Perceval
Script: Graham Greene
Origin: Original story by Graham Greene
Cast: Trevor Howard, Joseph Cotten, Alida Valli, Orson Welles
Running time: 93 minutes

1953   *The Heart of the Matter* (London Films)

Director: George More O'Ferrall
Producer: Ian Dalrymple
Script: Ian Dalrymple
Origin: Graham Greene's novel *The Heart of the Matter*
Cast: Trevor Howard, Elizabeth Allan, Maria Schell
Running time: 105 minutes

1954   *The Stranger's Hand/La Mano Dello Straniero* (John Stafford Pro-
        ductions for British Lion)

Director: Mario Soldati
Producer: John Stafford and Peter Moore, in association with
    Graham Greene
Script: Guy Elmes, Georgio Bassani
Origin: Original story by Graham Greene
Cast: Trevor Howard, Alida Valli, Richard Basehart, Richard
    O'Sullivan
Running time: 85 minutes

1955   *The End of the Affair* (Columbia Pictures, Coronado)

> Director: Edward Dmytryk
> Producer: David E. Rose
> Script: Lenore Coffee
> Origin: Graham Greene's novel *The End of the Affair*
> Cast: Deborah Kerr, Van Johnson, John Mills
> Running time: 105 minutes

1956   *Loser Takes All* (John Stafford Productions for British Lion)

> Director: Ken Annakin
> Producer: John Stafford
> Script: Graham Greene
> Origin: Graham Greene's novel *Loser Takes All*
> Cast: Glynis Johns, Rossano Brazzi, Robert Morley
> Running time: 88 minutes

1957   *Across the Bridge* (John Stafford Productions for J. Arthur Rank)

> Director: Ken Annakin
> Producer: John Stafford
> Script: Guy Elmes, Denis Freeman
> Origin: Graham Greene's story "Across the Bridge"
> Cast: Rod Steiger, Marla Landi, David Knight
> Running time: 103 minutes

1957   *The Quiet American* (United Artists, Figaro)

> Director: Joseph L. Mankiewicz
> Producer: Joseph L. Mankiewicz
> Script: Joseph L. Mankiewicz
> Origin: Graham Greene's novel *The Quiet American*
> Cast: Audie Murphy, Michael Redgrave, Claude Dauphin
> Running time: 121 minutes

1957   *Saint Joan* (Wheel Productions)

> Director: Otto Preminger
> Producer: Otto Preminger
> Script: Graham Greene
> Origin: George Bernard Shaw's play *Saint Joan*
> Cast: Jean Seberg, Anton Walbrook, Richard Widmark, John
>   Gielgud
> Running time: 109 minutes

1957 *Short Cut to Hell* (Paramount Pictures)

Director: James Cagney
Producer: A. C. Lyles
Script: Ted Berkman, Raphael Blau, W. R. Burnett
Origin: Graham Greene's novel *A Gun for Sale*
Cast: Robert Ivers, Georgann Johnson, William Bishop
Running time: 89 minutes

1959 *Our Man in Havana* (Kingsmead Productions, Columbia Pictures)

Director: Carol Reed
Producer: Carol Reed
Script: Graham Greene
Origin: Graham Greene's novel *Our Man in Havana*
Cast: Alec Guinness, Noel Coward, Ernie Kovacs
Running time: 111 minutes

1961 *The Power and the Glory* (David Suskind, CBS Television)

Director: Marc Daniels
Producer: David Suskind
Script: Dale Wasserman
Origin: Graham Greene's novel *The Power and the Glory*
Cast: Laurence Olivier, Julie Harris, George C. Scott
Running Time: 98 minutes

1967 *The Comedians* (Maximilian Productions, Metro-Goldwyn-Mayer)

Director: Peter Glenville
Producer: Peter Glenville
Script: Graham Greene
Origin: Graham Greene's novel *The Comedians*
Cast: Elizabeth Taylor, Richard Burton, Lillian Gish, Paul Ford,
    Alec Guinness
Running time: 156 minutes

1972   *Travels with My Aunt* (Metro-Goldwyn-Mayer)

> Director: George Cukor
> Producer: Robert Fryer and James Cresson
> Script: Jay Presson Allen and Hugh Wheeler
> Origin: Graham Greene's novel *The Comedians*
> Cast: Maggie Smith, Alec McCowen, Lou Gossett, Robert Stephens
> Running time: 109 minutes

1973   *England Made Me* (Atlantic Productions)

> Director: Peter Duffell
> Producer: Jack Levin
> Script: Peter Duffell and Desmond Cory
> Origin: Graham Greene's novel *England Made Me*
> Cast: Peter Finch, Michael York, Hildegard Neil
> Running time: 100 minutes

1980   *The Human Factor* (United Artists)

> Director: Otto Preminger
> Producer: Otto Preminger
> Script: Tom Stoppard
> Origin: Graham Greene's novel *The Human Factor*
> Cast: Nicol Williamson, Iman, Derek Jacobi, Robert Morley, Richard Attenborough, John Gielgud
> Running time: 120 minutes

1983   *The Honorary Consul* (U.S. title *Beyond the Limit*)
        (World Film Services for Paramount Pictures)

> Director: John MacKenzie
> Producer: Norman Heyman
> Script: Christopher Hampton
> Origin: Graham Greene's novel *The Honorary Consul*
> Cast: Richard Gere, Michael Caine, Bob Hoskins
> Running Time: 103 minutes

In Production

Doctor Fischer of Geneva (expected November, 1985)
Director: Lindsay Hogg
Producer: Richard Broke, BBC
Script: Richard Broke
Origin: Graham Greene's novel *Doctor Fischer of Geneva*

Selected
Bibliography

A complete bibliography of Greene's work, by Neil Brennan and the late Alan Redway, is forthcoming by Oxford University Press. Ronald Wobbe, *Graham Greene: A Bibliography and Guide to Research* (New York: Garland Publishing, 1979) is exhaustive up to the last few years. The books of Greene cited below are those quoted from in the text; a complete list of his *Spectator* and *Night and Day* film reviews between 1935 and 1940 appears in Wobbe. With the exception of a few relevant articles, the selection of critical works is limited to full-length studies.

By Graham Greene

Books

Brighton Rock. London: William Heinemann and Bodley Head, 1970.
British Dramatists. London: William Collins, 1942.
Collected Essays. New York: Viking Press, 1969.
The Comedians. London: Bodley Head, 1966.

The Confidential Agent. London: William Heinemann and Bodley Head, 1971.
The End of the Affair. London: William Heinemann, 1957.
England Made Me. London: William Heinemann, 1960.
A Gun for Sale. London: William Heinemann, 1947.
The Heart of the Matter. London: William Heinemann, 1965.
The Honorary Consul. London: Bodley Head, 1973.
It's a Battlefield. London: William Heinemann, 1956.
Journey Without Maps. London: William Heinemann, 1962.
The Lawless Roads. London: Longmans, Green and Co., 1939.
The Man Within. New York: Doubleday, Doran and Co., 1929.
The Ministry of Fear. New York: Viking Press, 1943.
Monsignor Quixote. Toronto: Lester and Orpen Dennys, 1982.
The Name of Action. London: William Heinemann, 1930.
Our Man in Havana. London: William Heinemann and Bodley Head, 1970.
The Portable Graham Greene. Edited by Philip Stratford. New York: Viking Press, 1973.
The Power and the Glory. London: William Heinemann and Bodley Head, 1971.
The Quiet American. London: William Heinemann, 1955.
Rumour at Nightfall. London: William Heinemann, 1931.
A Sort of Life. London: Bodley Head, 1971.
Stamboul Train. London: William Heinemann, 1951.
The Third Man (film script, with Carol Reed). London: Lorrimer Publishing, 1969.
The Third Man and The Fallen Idol. London: William Heinemann, 1950.
Travels with My Aunt. London: Bodley Head, 1969.
Ways of Escape. Toronto: Lester and Orpen Dennys, 1980.
With Elizabeth Bowen and V. S. Pritchett. *Why Do I Write?* London: Percival Marshall, 1948.

Articles

"The Art of Fiction." *Paris Review*, no. 3 (Autumn, 1953).
"The Average Film." *Oxford Outlook* 2, no. 32 (1925).
"The Camera Eye." *Spectator* 155 (September 27, 1935).
"Cinema." *Spectator* 155–64 (July 5, 1935–March 15, 1940).
"Dear Mr. Chaplin." *New Republic* 126 (October 13, 1952).
"The Films." *Night and Day* 1, nos. 1–26 (July 1, 1937–December 23, 1937).
"A Film Technique: Rhythms of Space and Time." *Times* (London), June 12, 1928.
"The Genius of Peter Lorre." *World Film News* 1, no. 4 (July, 1936).
"Is It Criticism?" *Sight and Sound* 5, no. 19 (Autumn, 1936).
"Middle-Brown Film." *Fortnightly Review* 139 (March 1936).
Graham Greene on Film. Edited by John Russell Taylor. New York: Simon and Schuster, 1972.
"The Novelist and the Cinema—A Personal Experience." In William Whitebait, ed. *International Film Annual: Number Two.* London: John Calder, 1958.
"Review of Films and Theatre." *Fortnightly Review* 140 (October, 1936).
"Sir Alexander Korda." *Sight and Sound* 25, no. 4 (Spring, 1956).
"A Stranger in the Theatre." *Picture Post*, April 18, 1953.
"Subjects and Stories." In Charles Davy, ed. *Footnotes to the Film.* London: Lovat Dickson, 1938.
"To Charlie Chaplin." *New Statesman and Nation*, April 27, 1952.

Unpublished Film Scripts

Unless otherwise indicated, the scripts are housed in the Humanities Research Center, University of Texas, Austin.

Brighton Rock
    Release Script, N.d. EMI-MGM Elstree Studios, Boreham Wood, England.
    "Second Film treatment," N.d. 79 pp.
    "Third Shooting Script," N.d. 114 pp.

The Comedians
    "Film Play." N.d. 91 pp.
    "Film Play." N.d. 293 pp.
    "Film Play: Story Line." N.d. 19 pp.
    "Film Play: Story Line—No. 2." N.d. 14 pp.
    "Film Play: Story Line—No. 3." N.d. 28 pp.
    "Film Play: Story Line—No. 4." N.d. 51 pp.
    "Motion Picture Version." N.d. 192 pp.
    "Motion Picture Version." N.d. 272 pp.
    "Motion Picture Version." N.d. 227 pp.
    "Screenplay—1." N.d. 165 pp.
    "Screenplay—2." July 1, 1966. 181 pp.
    "Screenplay—3." September 1, 1966. 170 pp.
    "Screenplay—4." December 1, 1966. 165 pp.

No Man's Land
    "Film Story." N.d. 30 pp.
    "Film Story Revised." N.d. 49 pp.

Our Man in Havana
    "Working Draft with Revisions." N.d. 177 pp.
    "Screenplay." January 12, 1959. 143 pp.

Saint Joan
    "First Draft." N.d. 107 pp.
    "Second Draft." N.d. 36 pp.
    "Third Draft." N.d. 90 pp.

The Stranger's Hand
    "Story." N.d. 30 pp.

The Tenth Man
    "Film treatment." N.d. 90 pp.

The Third Man
    "First Draft Script." N.d. 128 pp.
    "Release Script." N.d. 173 pp.
    "Second Draft Script." September 20, 1948. 98 pp.
    "Story." June 2, 1948. 127 pp.
    "Treatment." N.d. 120 pp.

Twenty-one Days
    "Release Script." N.d. British Film Institute Library, London.

Relevant Critical Works

Adamson, Judy. "Graham Greene as Film Critic." *Sight and Sound* 41, no. 2 (Spring, 1972).

————, and Philip Stratford. "Looking for the Third Man." *Encounter* 50, no. 6 (June, 1978).

Agee, James. *Agee on Film.* Vol. 1. New York: McDowell Obolensky, 1948.

Allain, Marie-Françoise. *The Other Man.* London: Bodley Head, 1983.

Appignanesi, Lisa. " Greeneland, Screenland." *Montreal Star,* April 4, 1970.

Auden, W. H., and John Garrett, eds. *The Poet's Tongue.* London: G. Bell and Sons, 1935.

Balcon, Michael, et al. *Twenty Years of British Film.* London: Falcon Press, 1947.

Bazin, André. *What Is Cinema?* Berkeley: University of California Press, 1975.

Behlmer, Rudy, ed. *Memo from: David O. Selznick.* New York: Avon books, 1973.

Bluestone, George. *Novels into Film.* Berkeley: University of California Press, 1968.

Bogdanovitch, Peter. *Fritz Lang in America.* London: Studio Vista, 1967.

————. *John Ford.* London: Studio Vista, 1968.

Branson, Noreen, and Margot Heinemann. *Britain in the Thirties.* London: Weidenfeld and Nicholson, 1971.

Butler, Ivan. *The Making of Feature Films.* London: Penguin Books, 1971.

Calder-Marshall, Arthur. *The Innocent Eye.* London: W. H. Allen, 1936; reprint, Baltimore, Md.: Penguin Books, 1963.

Clark, Jon, et al., eds. *Culture and Crisis in Britain in the 30's.* London: Lawrence and Wishart, 1979.

Consolo, Dominick. "Graham Greene: Style and Stylistics in Five Novels." In Robert O. Evans, ed. *Graham Greene: Some Critical Considerations.* Lexington: University of Kentucky Press, 1967.

Cooke, Alistair, ed. *Garbo and the Night Watchman.* London: Jonathan Cape, 1937.

Davies, Brenda, ed. *Carol Reed.* London: British Film Institute, 1978.

Davy, Charles, ed. *Footnotes to the Film.* London: Lovat Dickson, 1938.

Diephouse, Daniel. "Graham Greene and the Cinematic Imagination." Ph.D. diss. University of Michigan, 1978. University Microfilms International, Ann Arbor, Michigan.

Dukore, Bernard. *Saint Joan: A Screenplay by Bernard Shaw.* Seattle: University of Washington Press, 1968.

Eisenstein, Sergei. *Film Form.* New York: Harcourt, Brace and World, 1951.

Evans, Robert O., ed. *Graham Greene: Some Critical Considerations.* Lexington: University of Kentucky Press, 1967.

Galsworthy, John. *The Plays of John Galsworthy.* London: Duckworth, 1929.

Ginna, Robert. "Our Man in Havana." *Horizon* 2 (November, 1959).

Goodman, Ezra. "Carol Reed." *Theatre Arts* 21, no. 5 (May, 1947).

Grierson, John. *Grierson on the Movies.* Edited by Forsyth Hardy. London: Faber and Faber, 1981.

Hoggart, Richard. "The Force of Caricature: Aspects of the Art of Graham Greene," *Essays in Criticism* 3 (October, 1953).

Houston, Penelope. *The Contemporary Cinema, 1945–1963.* Middlesex: Penguin Books, 1963.

Hynes, Samuel. *The Auden Generation.* New York: Viking Press, 1977.

————, ed. *Graham Greene.* Englewood Cliffs, N.J.: Prentice-Hall, 1973.

Isherwood, Christopher. *Goodbye to Berlin.* London: Hogarth Press, 1960.

————. *Lions and Shadows.* Norfolk: New Directions, 1947.

Knight, Arthur. "Arthur Knight Interviews Mankiewicz." *Saturday Review,* January 21, 1958.

————. *The Liveliest Art*. New York: Mentor and Plume Books, 1957.

Korda, Michael. *Charmed Lives*. New York: Random House, 1979.

Lodge, David. *Graham Greene*. New York: Columbia University Press, 1966.

Low, Rachel. *Documentary and Educational Films of the 1930's*. London: George Allen and Unwin, 1979.

————. *Films of Comment and Persuasion of the 1930's*. London: George Allen and Unwin, 1979.

MacCann, Richard Dyer. *Film: A Montage of Theories*. New York: E. P. Dutton and Co., 1966.

Maddux, Rachel, et al. *Fiction into Film*. New York: Dell Publishing Co., 1970.

Magny, Claude-Edmonde. *The Age of the American Novel*. New York: Frederick Ungar Publishing Co., 1972.

Manvell, Roger, and John Huntley. *The Technique of Film Music*. London: Focal Press, 1957.

Mast, Gerald. *A Short History of the Movies*. New York: Bobbs Merrill Co., 1971.

Murray, Edward. *The Cinematic Imagination*. New York: Frederick Ungar Publishing Co., 1972.

Nicholson, Jenny. "Graham Greene—A 'Third Man' of Real Life." *Picture Post*, August 14, 1954.

Phillips, Gene D., S.J. Graham Greene: The Films of His Fiction. New York: Teacher's College Press, 1974.

————, ed. *Literature/Film Quarterly* 4, no. 4 (Fall, 1974).

Pratley, Gerald. *The Cinema of Otto Preminger*. London: C. Tinling and Co., 1971.

Republic of Haiti, Department of Foreign Affairs. *Graham Greene Finally Exposed*. Bulletin of the Department of Foreign Affairs. Port-au-Prince, 1968.

Richardson, Robert. *Literature and Film*. Bloomington and London: Indiana University Press, 1969.

Roberts, Michael. *New Signatures*. London: Hogarth Press, 1934.

Shaw, Bernard. *Saint Joan*. Middlesex: Penguin Books, 1973.

Spender, Stephen. *The New Realism*. London: Hogarth Press, 1939.

Spier, Ursula. "Melodrama in Graham Greene's *The End of the Affair*." *Modern Fiction Studies* 3 (Autumn, 1957).

Stratford, Philip. *Faith and Fiction*. Notre Dame, Ind: University of Notre Dame Press, 1964.

Wagner, Geoffrey. *The Novel and the Cinema*. Rutherford, N.J.: Fairleigh Dickinson University Press, 1975.

Waugh, Evelyn. "Felix Culpa?" *Tablet* 191 (June 5, 1948).

Woolf, Virginia. "The Movies and Reality." *New Republic* 47 (August 4, 1926).

Wright, Basil. "A Study of Carol Reed." In *The Year's Work in the Film: 1949*. London: Longmans, Green and Co., 1950.

Interviews

Boulting, John. London, October 7, 1970.

Greene, Graham. Antibes, October 28, 1970.

————. Antibes, June 21, 1982.

Grierson, John. Calstone, July 24, 1970.

Letters

Allen, Jay. New York, April 18, 1972.
Greene, Graham. Antibes, June 19, 1972.
————. Antibes, October 10, 1983.
Reid, Josephine. London, Undated.

Newspapers

Daily Express *Evening Standard*
Daily Graphic *Glasgow Herald*
Daily Herald *Observer*
Daily Mail *Listener*
Daily Mirror *Manchester Guardian*
Daily Telegraph *Sunday Times* (London)
Daily Worker *Times* (London)

Notes

Preface

1. John Russell Taylor, *Times* (London), January 20, 1968.
2. Gene D. Phillips, S.J., *Graham Greene: The Films of His Fiction*, p. xix.
3. André Bazin, *What Is Cinema?* p. 61.
4. Richard Hoggart, "The Force of Caricature," *Essays in Criticism* 3 (October, 1953):456.
5. Author's interview with John Boulting, October 7, 1970.
6. Herbert Read, "Towards a Film Aesthetic," in Richard Dyer MacCann, ed., *Film: A Montage of Theories*, p. 170.
7. Graham Greene, "Subjects and Stories," in Charles Davy, ed., *Footnotes to the Film*, p. 57.
8. Ibid.
9. John Grierson, *Grierson on the Movies*, ed. Forsyth Hardy, p. 91.

Chapter One

1. Graham Greene, *Ways of Escape*, pp. 43–44.
2. Ibid., p. 43.
3. Graham Greene, "Cinema," *Spectator* 155 (October 18, 1935):606.
4. Graham Greene, "Is It Criticism?" *Sight and Sound* 5, no. 19 (Autumn, 1936):650.

5. Graham Greene, "Review of Films and Theatre," *Fortnightly Review* 140 (October, 1936):380.

6. Graham Greene, *The Lawless Roads*, p. 10.

7. Graham Greene, *A Sort of Life*, p. 72.

8. Ibid., p. 17.

9. Greene, *The Lawless Roads*, pp. 10–12.

10. Graham Greene, *The Honorary Consul*, p. 205.

11. Greene, *A Sort of Life*, pp. 18–19.

12. Graham Greene, *Journey Without Maps*, p. 11.

13. Christopher Isherwood, Foreword, in Edward Upward, *The Railway Accident and Other Stories* (London: Penguin Books, 1972), p. 34.

14. Greene, *Journey Without Maps*, p. 10.

15. Ibid., pp. 7–10.

16. Ibid.

17. W. H. Auden, from *The Highway*, December, 1936, in Jon Clark et al., eds., *Culture and Crisis in Britain in the 30's*, p. 105.

18. Graham Greene, "The Novelist and the Cinema—A Personal Experience," in William Whitebait, ed., *International Film Annual: Number Two*, p. 56.

19. Graham Greene, "Subjects and Stories," in Charles Davy, ed., *Footnotes to the Film*, p. 68.

20. Graham Greene, *British Dramatists*, p. 26.

21. Ibid., pp. 26, 18.

22. Graham Greene, "Cinema," *Spectator* 155 (December 6, 1935):940.

23. Greene, "Review of Films and Theatre," *Fortnightly Review* 140 (October, 1936):380.

24. Graham Greene, "Cinema," *Spectator* 157 (August 14, 1936):270.

25. Ibid.

26. Ibid.

27. Graham Greene, "Cinema," *Spectator* 158 (February 26, 1937):356.

28. Ibid.

29. Ibid.

30. Aristotle, *The Poetics*, in Allan H. Gilbert, *Literary Criticism: Plato to Dryden* (Detroit, Mich.: Wayne State University Press, 1962), p. 108.

31. Greene, *Footnotes to the Film*, p. 61.

32. Ibid., p. 62.

33. Ibid., pp. 69–70.

34. Graham Greene, "Cinema," *Spectator* 155 (September 27, 1935):462.

35. Graham Greene, "Cinema," *Spectator* 156 (February 14, 1936):254.

36. Greene, *Footnotes to the Film*, p. 58.

37. Graham Greene, "Cinema," *Spectator* 156 (January 31, 1936):170.

38. Greene, *Footnotes to the Film*, p. 60.

39. Ibid., p. 62.

40. Arthur Calder-Marshall, *The Innocent Eye*, p. 97.

41. Graham Greene, "Cinema," *Spectator* 164 (February 16, 1940):213.

42. Greene, "Cinema," *Spectator* 155 (December 6, 1935):940.

43. Graham Greene, "Cinema," *Spectator* 162 (June 23, 1939):1088.

44. Greene, "Cinema," *Spectator* 155 (December 6, 1935):940.

45. Graham Greene, "Cinema," *Spectator* 157 (July 31, 1936):199.

46. Greene, *Footnotes to the Film*, p. 63.

47. Graham Greene, "The Cinema," *Night and Day* 1, no. 3 (July 15, 1937):30.

48. Graham Greene, "Cinema," *Spectator* 155 (July 19, 1935):94.

49. Graham Greene, "Cinema," *Spectator* 164 (January 26, 1940):108.

50. Graham Greene, "Cinema," *Spectator* 156 (February 7, 1936):211.

51. Graham Greene, "The Camera Eye," *Spectator* 155 (September 27, 1935):472.

52. Greene, *Footnotes to the Film*, p. 57.

53. Graham Greene, Elizabeth Bowen and V. S. Pritchett, *Why Do I Write?* p. 30.

54. Stephen Spender, *The New Realism*, p. 8.

55. Michael Roberts, *New Signatures*, p. 11.

56. Christopher Isherwood, *Lions and Shadows*, p. 86.

57. Christopher Isherwood, *Goodbye to Berlin*, p. 13.

58. Graham Greene, "The Virtue of Disloyalty," in Graham Greene, *The Portable Graham Greene*, ed. Philip Stratford, p. 609.

59. Graham Greene, "Review of Films and Theatre," *Fortnightly Review* 140 (October, 1936):380.

60. Greene, "Is It Criticism?" *Sight and Sound*, 5, no. 19 (Autumn, 1936):65.

61. Graham Greene, "Cinema," *Spectator* 156 (March 20, 1936):512.

62. Graham Greene, "The Films, " *Night and Day* 1, no. 15 (October 7, 1937):38.

63. Graham Greene, "The Films," *Night and Day* 1, no. 19 (November 4, 1937):31.

64. Greene, "The Films," *Night and Day* 1, no. 15 (October 7, 1937):38.

65. Graham Greene, "Cinema," *Spectator* 156 (June 5, 1936):1036.

66. Graham Greene, "Cinema," *Spectator* 164. (February 9, 1940):179.

67. Graham Greene, "Cinema," *Spectator* 157 (August 7, 1936):235.

68. *Times* (London), March 22, 1938, p. 5.

69. Godfrey Winn, "Godfrey Winn's Personality Parade," *Daily Mirror* (London), November 2, 1937, p. 11.

70. Author's interview with Graham Greene, October 28, 1970.

71. *Times* (London), March 22, 1938, p. 5.

72. Information for the above six paragraphs is taken from Michael Balcon, "The British Film Today," in Michael Balcon et al., *Twenty Years of British Film*, pp. 13–28.

73. Graham Greene, "Cinema," *Spectator* 164 (April 21, 1939):668.

74. Graham Greene, "Cinema," *Spectator* 164 (April 7, 1939):592.

75. Greene, *Ways of Escape*, p. 6.

76. Ibid., pp. 4–6.

77. Ibid., p. 8.

78. Ibid., p. 9.

79. Ibid., p. 10.

80. Graham Greene, *Brighton Rock*, pp. 102–03.

81. Graham Greene, *The Man Within*, pp. 236–37.

82. Graham Greene, *Rumour at Nightfall*, p. 44.

83. Ibid. p. 4.

84. Ibid., p. 277.

85. Greene, *Brighton Rock*, p. 204.

86. Greene, *The Man Within*, pp. 222–32.

87. Graham Greene, *The Name of Action*, p. 248.

88. Graham Greene, *Stamboul Train*, pp. 144–46.

89. Graham Greene, *It's a Battlefield*, pp. 143–44.

90. Greene, *Brighton Rock*, pp. 225–26.

91. Graham Greene, *Ways of Escape*, pp. 16–19.

92. Graham Greene, "Cinema," *Spectator* 155 (December 6, 1935):940.

93. Gene D. Phillips, S.J., *Graham Greene: The Films of His Fiction*, p. 15.

94. Sergei Eisenstein, *Film Form*, p. 238.

95. Author's interview with John Grierson, July 24, 1970.

96. W. H. Auden, Introduction, in W. H. Auden and John Garrett, eds., *The Poet's Tongue*, p. ix.

97. Greene, *Footnotes to the Film*, p. 61.

Chapter Two

1. Graham Greene, *Ways of Escape*, p. 49.

2. Author's interview with Graham Greene, October 28, 1970.

3. Greene, *Ways of Escape*, p. 49.

4. Ibid.

5. Graham Greene, "The Novelist and the Cinema—A Personal Experience," in William Whitebait, ed., *International Film Annual: Number Two*, p. 55.

6. Graham Greene, *Journey Without Maps*, p. 19.

7. Graham Greene, "The Novelist and the Cinema," p. 55.

8. Ibid.

9. Ibid., p. 54.

10. Graham Greene, "The Art of Fiction," *Paris Review*, no. 3 (Autumn, 1953):40.

11. Graham Greene, "Cinema," *Spectator* 164 (January 12, 1940):44.

12. Greene, "The Novelist and the Cinema," p. 56.

13. John Galsworthy, *The Plays of John Galsworthy*, pp. 920–21.

14. Greene, "The Novelist and the Cinema," p. 56.

15. Greene, "Cinema," *Spectator* 164 (January 12, 1940):44.

16. Author's interview with Greene, October 28, 1970.

17. Greene, "Cinema," *Spectator* 164 (January 12, 1940):44.

18. Graham Greene, "The Lieutenant Died Last," in Hugh Greene, ed., *The Pirate of the Round Pond*, (London: Bodley Head, 1977), p. 22.

19. James Agee, *Agee on Film*, 1:104.

20. Norman Lebrecht, "The Greene Factor," *Sunday Times* (London), April 1, 1984, p. 34. Lebrecht quotes Greene as saying he had forgotten that he had written *The Tenth Man*. He thought it was something he had "jotted down on two sheets of notepaper." When he discovered MGM had sold the manuscript to Anthony Blond, a British publisher, for £8000, Greene planned to "use all kinds of blackmail to stop it being published." But then to his "disquiet" he found it "rather good, in fact rather better than *The Third Man*," and agreed to its being printed. It will appear, Lebrecht says in "Found: Graham Greene's Lost Novel" (page 1 of the same edition of the *Sunday Times*), with an introduction in which Greene will reveal the identity of "another film treatment he wrote [presumably during the same period] which MGM made into an important movie. Its identity is being withheld until publication . . . [in February, 1985] to tantalise Greene's readers," we are told.

21. Greene, *Ways of Escape*, p. 81.

22. Peter Bogdanovitch, *Fritz Lang in America*, p. 65.

23. Lisa Appignanesi, "Greeneland, Screenland," *Montreal Star* April 4, 1970, p. 4.

24. Agee, *Agee on Film*, 1:178–79.

25. G. H. Lewes, "Dickens in Relation to Criticism," *Fortnightly Review*, February 1, 1872, p. 149.

26. Author's interview with Greene, October 28, 1970.

27. "Graham Greene Takes the Orient Express," *Listener*, November 21, 1968, pp. 672–73.

28. Graham Greene, *The Confidential Agent*, p. 80.

29. Graham Greene, *The Power and the Glory*, p. 202.

30. Greene, *The Confidential Agent*, p. 149.

31. Graham Greene, *The Third Man and The Fallen Idol*, p. 66.

32. Ibid., p. 174.

33. Ibid., p. 179.

34. Virginia Woolf, "The Movies and Reality," *New Republic* 47 (August 4, 1926):309.

35. Graham Greene, *The Travel Books of Graham Greene* (London: Mercury Books, 1963), p. 207.

36. Ibid., p. 124.

37. Greene, *The Confidential Agent*, pp. 3–4.

38. Agee, *Agee on Film*, 1:178–79.

39. Greene, *Ways of Escape*, p. 6.

40. *News Chronicle*, April 3, 1948.

41. Greene, "The Novelist and the Cinema," p. 55.

42. *Times* (London) April 5, 1948.

43. Author's interview with John Boulting, October 7, 1970.

44. Graham Greene, *Brighton Rock*, p. 1.

45. Greene, *Ways of Escape*, pp. 61–62.

46. Greene, *Brighton Rock*. p. 280.

47. Ibid., p. 204.

48. Ibid., p. 310.

49. Ibid., p. 304.

50. Ibid., p. 307.

51. Graham Greene, *Brighton Rock* (film), "Second Film Treatment" (Humanities Research Center, University of Texas, Austin, n.d.); "Release Script" (EMI-MGM Elstree Studios, Boreham Wood, England, n.d.).

52. Author's interview with Greene, October 28, 1970.

53. Graham Greene, *Daily Mirror* (London), January 9, 1948.

54. Author's interview with Boulting, October 7, 1970.

55. Reg Whitley, *Daily Mirror*, January 8, 1948.

56. Author's interview with Boulting, October 7, 1970.

57. Graham Greene, *Daily Mirror*, January 9, 1948.

58. Author's interview with Greene, October 28, 1970.

59. Greene, *Brighton Rock*, p. 304.

Chapter Three

1. Graham Greene, "Cinema," *Spectator* 156 (January 3, 1936):14.

2. Graham Greene, "Cinema," *Spectator* 156 (January 3, 1936):14.

3. Graham Greene, "Cinema," *Spectator* 164 (January 26, 1940):108.

4. Graham Greene, "Cinema," *Spectator* 157 (July 31, 1936):199.

5. Graham Greene, *The Third Man and The Fallen Idol*, p. 145.

6. Ibid., p. 173.

7. Ibid., p. 146.

8. Greene, "Cinema," *Spectator* 156 (January 3, 1936):14.

9. Ezra Goodman, "Carol Reed," *Theatre Arts* 21, no. 5 (May, 1947):57.

10. Charles T. Samuels, "Interview with Carol Reed," in Brenda Davies, ed. *Carol Reed*, p. 10.

11. Greene, *The Third Man and The Fallen Idol*, p. 4.

12. Ibid., p. 146.

13. Dilys Powell, "The Fallen Idol," *Sunday Times* (London), March 10, 1948.
14. Ibid.
15. Graham Greene, "Cinema," *Spectator* 156 (May 1, 1936):791.
16. Goodman, "Carol Reed," p. 57.
17. Ibid., p. 58.
18. Greene, *The Third Man and The Fallen Idol*, p. 171.
19. Greene, "Cinema," *Spectator* 157 (July 31, 1936):199.
20. Greene, *The Third Man and The Fallen Idol*, pp. 157–58.
21. Ibid., p. 155.
22. Goodman, "Carol Reed," p. 57.
23. Greene, *The Third Man and The Fallen Idol*, pp. 155–56.
24. Gene D. Phillips, S.J., *Graham Greene: The Films of His Fiction*, p. 51.
25. Greene, *The Third Man and The Fallen Idol*, p. 158.
26. Ibid., p. 22.
27. Ibid., p. 3.
28. Ibid.
29. Graham Greene, *Ways of Escape*, p. 106.
30. Ibid., p. 107.
31. Ibid., p. 106.
32. Greene, *The Third Man and The Fallen Idol*, p. 4.
33. Ibid.
34. Jenny Nicholson, "Graham Greene—A 'Third Man' of Real Life," *Picture Post*, August 14, 1954, p. 19.
35. Greene, *Ways of Escape*, p. 105.
36. Greene, *The Third Man and The Fallen Idol*, p. 5.
37. Ibid.
38. Ibid., pp. 5–6.
39. Ibid., pp. 68–69.
40. Ibid., p. 95.
41. Ibid., p. 127.
42. Greene, *Ways of Escape*. p. 50.
43. Ibid., p. 51.
44. Rudy Behlmer, ed., *Memo from: David O. Selznick*, p. 447.
45. Greene, *The Third Man and The Fallen Idol*, p. 6.
46. Greene (with Reed), *The Third Man*, pp. 102–103.
47. Ibid., p. 106.
48. Greene, *Ways of Escape*, p. 105.
49. Greene, *The Third Man and The Fallen Idol*, p. 6.
50. Author's interview with Greene, June 21, 1982.
51. *Manchester Guardian*, March 11, 1950.
52. Greene, *Ways of Escape*, p. 105.
53. Greene, *The Third Man and The Fallen Idol*, p. 8.
54. Greene (with Reed), *The Third Man*, p. 124.
55. Behlmer, ed., *Memo from: David O. Selznick*, p. 452.
56. Ibid., p. 458.
57. Greene, *Ways of Escape*, p. 52.
58. John Grierson, *Grierson on the Movies*, p. 91.

Chapter Four

1. Letter from Graham Greene to author, June 19, 1972.
2. Graham Greene, *Ways of Escape*, p. 118.
3. Graham Greene, *No Man's Land*, "Film Story" (Humanities Research Center, University of Texas, Austin, (n.d.).
4. Greene, *Ways of Escape*, pp. 113–14.
5. Ibid., p. 114.
6. Ibid.
7. Ibid., p. 140.
8. Graham Greene, *The Quiet American*, p. 17.
9. Ibid., p. 205.
10. Graham Greene, *The End of the Affair*, p. 1.
11. Ibid.
12. Greene, *The Quiet American*, p. 27.
13. Graham Greene, *The Comedians*, p. 9–10.
14. Greene, *The Quiet American*, p. 23.
15. Dominick Consolo, "Graham Greene: Style and Stylistics in Five Novels," in Robert O. Evans, ed., *Graham Greene: Some Critical Considerations*. In my account of Greene's narrative method here and in Chap. 5, I owe much to Consolo's article and to Daniel Diephouse, "Graham Greene and the Cinematic Imagination" (Ph.D. diss., University of Michigan, 1978).
16. Greene, *Ways of Escape*, p. 126.
17. Ibid., pp. 163–64.
18. Ibid., pp. 157–58.
19. Ibid., p. 108.
20. Ibid.
21. Ibid., p. 174.
22. Graham Greene, "The Novelist and the Cinema—A Personal Experience," in William Whitebait, ed., *International Film Annual: Number Two*, p. 61.
23. *Manchester Guardian*, April 27, 1951.
24. *Daily Telegraph*, January 13, 1954.
25. *Times* (London), December 30, 1953.
26. Greene, "The Novelist and the Cinema," p. 61.
27. Author's interview with Graham Greene, October 28, 1970.
28. *Glasgow Herald*, August 23, 1954.
29. The manuscript for the first draft with revisions of *The Stranger's Hand* is in the Humanities Research Center, Austin (n.d.).
30. Author's interview with Greene, October 28, 1970.
31. Greene, "The Novelist and the Cinema," p. 61.
32. William Whitebait, *New Statesman*, July 3, 1954.
33. *Daily Express*, June 4, 1954.
34. *New Statesman*, July 3, 1954.
35. *Sunday Times* (London), June 6, 1954.
36. *Glasgow Herald*, August 23, 1954.
37. Greene, *Ways of Escape*, p. 186.
38. Ibid., p. 187.
39. Thomas Wiseman, *Evening Standard*, August 8, 1953.
40. Author's interview with Greene, October 28, 1970.
41. Greene, *Ways of Escape*, p. 187.

42. C. A. Lejune, *Observer*, November 18, 1956.

43. *Times* (London), November 19, 1956.

44. Fred Majdalany, *Daily Mail*, November 16, 1956.

45. Ibid.

46. Author's interview with Greene, June 21, 1982.

47. Graham Greene, "The Novelist and the Cinema," p. 61.

48. Roderick Mann, *Daily Graphic*, January 10, 1952.

49. Greene, *Ways of Escape*, p. 180.

50. Graham Greene, "Dear Mr. Chaplin," *New Republic*, October 13, 1952, p. 5.

51. Greene, *Ways of Escape*, p. 115.

52. N. Graham, *Spectator*, March 4, 1955.

53. Gene D. Phillips, S.J., *Graham Greene: The Films of His Fiction*, pp. 131–32.

54. Greene, *Ways of Escape*, p. 116.

55. Greene, "The Novelist and the Cinema," p. 55.

56. Nina Hibbin, *Daily Worker*, March 29, 1958.

57. L. Mosley, *Daily Express*, March 26, 1958.

58. Dilys Powell, *Sunday Times*, March 21, 1958.

59. Arthur Knight, "Arthur Knight Interviews Mankiewicz," *Saturday Review*, January 21, 1958.

60. Leslie Mallory, "Leslie Mallory Interviews Redgrave," *News Chronicle*, March 20, 1958.

61. Greene, "The Novelist and the Cinema," p. 55.

62. Ibid., p. 56.

63. Gerald Pratley, *The Cinema of Otto Preminger*, p. 120.

64. Bernard Shaw, *Saint Joan*, p. 64.

65. Author's interview with Graham Greene, June 21, 1982.

66. Gerald Pratley, *The Cinema of Otto Preminger*, pp. 117–19.

67. Bernard Dukore, *Saint Joan: A Screenplay by Bernard Shaw* (Seattle: University of Washington Press, 1968), p. xxxvii. A complete list of the censor's proposed deletions and changes is found in ibid., appendix B.

68. Author's interview with Graham Greene, October 28, 1970; Pratley, *The Cinema of Otto Preminger*, p. 118. The two manuscripts for the screenplay of *Saint Joan* are in the British Library. The first is dated 1934; the second is undated.

69. Phillips, *Graham Greene*, p. 46.

70. Author's interview with Greene, June 21, 1982.

71. Greene, *Ways of Escape*, pp. 199–200.

72. *Daily Express*, November 10, 1958.

73. Greene, *Ways of Escape*, pp. 205–207.

74. Lisa Appignanesi, "Greeneland, Screenland," *Montreal Star*, April 4, 1970, p. 4.

75. *Daily Express*, April 16, 1959.

76. *Daily Mail*, April 16, 1959.

77. Graham Greene, *Our Man in Havana*, pp. 61–62.

78. Ibid. p. 30.

79. Philip Stratford, *Faith and Fiction*, p. 324.

80. Robert Muller, *Daily Mail*, December 30, 1959.

81. Dilys Powell, *Sunday Times* (London) February 2, 1960.

82. Phillips, *Graham Greene*, p. 86.

83. Greene, *Our Man in Havana*, p. 125.

84. Ibid., pp. 153–55.

85. Phillips, *Graham Greene*, pp. 85–86.

86. Robert Gina, "Our Man in Havana," *Horizon* 2 (November, 1959):122.
87. Author's interview with Greene, June 21, 1982.
88. Arthur Knight, *The Liveliest Art*, p. 219.
89. Penelope Houston, *The Contemporary Cinema, 1945–1963*, p. 11.
90. Gerald Mast, *A Short History of the Movies*, pp. 333.

Chapter Five

1. Graham Greene, "The Novelist and the Cinema—A Personal Experience," in William Whitebait, ed., *International Film Annual: Number Two*, p. 61.
2. Graham Greene, *Ways of Escape*, p. 58.
3. Graham Greene, *It's a Battlefield*, p. 119.
4. Ibid., p. 223.
5. Graham Greene, *A Gun for Sale*, p. 13.
6. Graham Greene, *England Made Me*, p. 50.
7. Graham Greene, *Stamboul Train*, p. 49.
8. Greene, *England Made Me*, p. 238.
9. Graham Greene, *The Ministry of Fear*, p. 64.
10. Ibid., p. 3.
11. Ibid., p. 63.
12. Ibid., p. 66.
13. Ibid., p. 90.
14. Ibid., p. 73.
15. Graham Greene, *Brighton Rock*, pp. 248, 206.
16. Ibid., p. 248.
17. Graham Greene, *Collected Essays*, pp. 49–50.
18. Graham Greene, "Cinema," *Spectator* 156 (April 24, 1936):766.
19. Graham Greene, *The Power and the Glory*, p. 79.
20. Ibid., pp. 81–83.
21. Graham Greene, *The Heart of the Matter*, pp. 306–307.
22. Ibid. pp. 314, 316.
23. Greene, *A Gun for Sale*, p. 111.
24. Greene, *The Power and the Glory*, pp. 19–20.
25. Ibid., p. 66.
26. Ibid., p. 144.
27. Ibid., pp. 1–2.
28. Ibid., p. 1.
29. Ibid., p. 3.
30. Ibid., p. 7.
31. Graham Greene, *The End of the Affair*, pp. 156–57.
32. Graham Greene, *Rumour at Nightfall*, pp. 276–77.
33. Greene, *Stamboul Train*, p. 132.
34. Greene, *Brighton Rock*, p. 301.
35. Greene, *The Power and the Glory*, pp. 205, 114.
36. Greene, *The Heart of the Matter*, p. 67.
37. Graham Greene, Collected Essays, p. 117.
38. Graham Greene, *Ways of Escape*, p. 51.
39. Ibid., pp. 233–34.
40. Ibid., p. 51.
41. Peter Bogdanovich, *John Ford*, p. 86.

Chapter Six

1. Graham Greene, *The Comedians*, p. 46.
2. Ibid., p. 9.
3. Ibid., p. 177.
4. Ibid., p. 310.
5. Ibid., p. 105.
6. Ibid., p. 304.
7. Ibid., p. 5.
8. Ibid., p. 304.
9. Gene D. Phillips, S.J., *Graham Greene: The Films of His Fiction*, p. 182.
10. Greene, *The Comedians*, p. 229.
11. Ibid., p. 307.
12. Ibid., p. 312.
13. Ibid., p. 306.
14. Ibid., p. 312.
15. Ibid., p. 290.
16. Ibid., p. 177.
17. *Graham Greene Finally Exposed*, Republic of Haiti, Department of Foreign Affairs, Bulletin of the Department of Foreign Affairs (1968), pp. 17, 39, 87, 39, foreword.
18. Ibid., pp. 59, 97.
19. Author's interview with Graham Greene, October 28, 1970.
20. *New York Times*, October 30, 1971, p. 63.
21. Graham Greene, *Ways of Escape*, p. 232.
22. Author's interview with Graham Greene, June 21, 1982.
23. Ivan Butler, *The Making of Feature Films*, p. 44.
24. Ibid.
25. Dilys Powell, *Sunday Times* (London), January 21, 1968.
26. Andrew Sarris, *Village Voice*, December 14, 1967.
27. Arthur Knight, *Saturday Review*, October 28, 1967.
28. Ian Christie, *Daily Express*, January 17, 1968.
29. Author's interview with Greene, October 28, 1970.
30. Graham Greene, *Travels with My Aunt*, pp. 10–11.
31. Ibid., pp. 307, 318.
32. Author's interview with Greene, June 21, 1982.
33. Letter from Jay Allen to author, April 18, 1972.
34. Geoffrey Wagner, *The Novel and the Cinema*, p. 27.
35. Author's interview with Greene, June 21, 1982.
36. Ibid.
37. Ibid.
38. Author's interview with Greene, June 21, 1982.
39. Graham Greene, *Ways of Escape*. p. 255.
40. Ibid., p. 257.
41. Letter from Graham Greene to author, October 10, 1983.
42. Letter from Josephine Reed (secretary to Graham Greene) to author (n.d.).
43. Author's interview with Greene, June 21, 1982.

Chapter Seven

1. Graham Greene, *A Sort of Life*, p. 11.
2. Graham Greene, *Ways of Escape*, p. 62.

3. Graham Greene, "A Stranger in the Theatre," *Picture Post*, April 18, 1953, p. 18.

4. Graham Greene, "The Novelist and the Cinema—A Personal Experience," in William Whitebait, ed., *International Film Annual: Number Two*, pp. 55–61.

5. Author's interview with Graham Greene, June 21, 1982.

6. Greene, *Ways of Escape*, p. 200.

7. Author's interview with Graham Greene, June 21, 1982.

8. Ibid.

9. Graham Greene [unsigned but acknowledged, October 23, 1970], "A Film Technique: Rhythms of Space and Time," *Times* (London), June 12, 1928, p. 14.

10. Graham Greene, "Cinema," *Spectator* 155 (December 6, 1935):940.

11. Greene, "The Novelist and the Cinema," p. 56.

12. Graham Greene, *Picture Post*, April 18, 1953, p. 19.

13. Graham Greene, "Cinema," *Spectator* 156 (January 24, 1936):137.

14. Graham Greene, "Cinema," *Spectator* 162 (May 26, 1939):901.

15. Author's interview with Greene, June 21, 1982.

16. Graham Greene, Elizabeth Bowen, and V. S. Pritchett, *Why Do I Write?* p. 50.

17. Graham Greene, "Cinema," *Spectator* 155, (December 20, 1935):1028.

18. Graham Greene, *Footnotes to the Film*, p. 60.

19. Author's interview with Greene, June 21, 1982.

20. Ibid.

21. Ibid.

22. Ibid.

23. Ibid.

24. Graham Greene, *Monsignor Quixote*, p. 37.

25. Author's interview with Greene, June 21, 1982.

26. Julian Symons, *Times Literary Supplement*, October 8, 1982.

27. Author's interview with Greene, June 21, 1982.

28. Evelyn Waugh, "Felix Culpa?" *Tablet* 191 (June 5, 1948):353.

29. Graham Greene, "The Novelist and the Cinema," p. 56.

30. Author's interview with Greene, June 21, 1982.

Index

187